i

# The Art of Poetry volume 3

## Forward: *Poems of the Decade anthology*

Published by Peripeteia Press Ltd.

First published April 2016

ISBN: 978-0-9930778-8-3

Peripeteia.webs.com

# Contents

# General Introduction to the The Art of Poetry series

The philosopher Nietzsche described his work as 'the greatest gift that (mankind) has ever been given'. The Elizabethan poet Edmund Spencer hoped his book **The Faerie Queene** would transform its readers into noblemen. In comparison, our aims for *The Art of Poetry* series of books are a little more modest. Fundamentally we aim to provide books that will be of maximum use to English students and their teachers. In our experience few students before A-level, and not all students at this level, read essays on poetry, yet, whatever specification they are studying, they have to write analytical essays on poetry. So, we've offering some models, written in a lively and accessible style. In Volume 1 we chose canonical poems for a number of reasons: Firstly they are simply great poems, well worth reading and studying; secondly we chose poems from across time so that they sketch in outline major developments in English poetry, from the Elizabethan period up until the present day. And, being canonical poems, they often crop up on GCSE and A-level specifications, so our material will be useful critical accompaniment and revision material.

This current book, volume 3 is, however, dedicated to modern poetry, in particular, to the **Forward Poems of the Decade** anthology. Hence, taken as a whole, **The Art of Poetry** series will cover a rich and varied range of literature, from poems that have endured years of critical readings to ones on which very little has been written, until now that is. The introductions that follow expand on and develop ideas first explored in volume 2.

1

# Introduction to *Volume 3: Poems of the Decade*

Our primary audience for this book is A-level students, but we've included teaching ideas that we hope might be of use to colleagues. (We've used the

 utterly unoriginal, but universally understood sign of the light bulb to signify a teaching idea. At the back of the book there's also a list of tried and tested revision activities which can be completed individually or with a class.) It's a brave step for English teachers to choose this anthology; there are no 'how

to teach' guides or (currently) York Notes, or such like, for this text; the onus is on the expertise and creativity of teachers to make this text work in a classroom. Fortunately, though I say it myself as a practising English teacher, English teachers enjoy these kinds of creative challenge and are usually very good at them. Perhaps a little support will, we hope, be useful.

Edexcel's exam questions require comparison of poems both at AS and A-level. At AS students will have a choice of two questions, each of which will ask them to compare a poem of their choice with one chosen by the Edexcel examiners. Unsurprisingly, at A-level the task is a little stiffer. Here a poem from the Forward anthology will have to be compared with an 'unseen' poem. As teachers, we are well aware of the demands of writing about 'unseen' material, so in the third section of this introduction we offer some advice about how to tackle the unseen. We'll also go on to say a few things about comparing texts.

\*\*\*\*\*\*\*\*

Self-evidently Forward's is a very modern poetry anthology; all the poems it contains were published in the twenty-first century. What might a gentleman poet from a hundred or so years ago make of this collection? What would be likely to surprise him, both in terms of the poetry itself and of the society it depicts? What might he find most peculiar, challenging, perhaps even shocking? To be a little more precise, what might our imaginary gentleman make of Edexcel's selection from the Forward anthology collection?

Our guess is that the first thing our imaginary poet would notice is the number of female poets included. About half of these poems were written by women. How many famous female poets in total could you name before studying this anthology? Honestly. Perhaps Emily Dickinson, Sylvia Plath, Carol Ann Duffy. Maybe you'll be able to think of more, but most people, including English teachers, could probably name precious few. You might counter that few male poets are well known today either, such is the low status of poetry in our culture. Perhaps. But we reckon names such as Shakespeare, Wordsworth, Shelley, Tennyson, Wilfred Owen and co are still pretty widely recognised. The gender balance in Edexcel's selection reflects a more equal society in which women are often at least as well educated as men, especially so in the literary arts.

Schooled in the Victorian concept of the two spheres, the masculine sphere of action and the feminine sphere of domesticity, our imaginary poet might expect poetry written by women to be expressed in suitably genteel language and to concern itself predominantly with domestic matters. If so, he'd be in for a shock. Certainly a number of these poems explore close family relationships, such as those between parents and children. Morrissey's *Genetics*, Boland's *Inheritance* and Barber's *Material* spring to mind. But the same topic is explored by male poets, such as Jenkins in *Effects*, Heaney in *Out of the Bag* and Thorpe in *On her Blindness*. The subject of family doesn't appear to be gendered. And though the poets explore issues of home and family life they do so in ways that would surely surprise and probably shock our imaginary reader: The fierce, unflinching narration of Doshi's *The Deliverer*, its direct depiction of brutality; Agbabi's disturbing portrayal of a relationship in *Eat Me* that ends in an act of cannibalism; the erotic thrill Feaver's narrator feels in *The Gun* from the close presence of blood and death - none of these poets shy away from life in the raw or show any concern for poetic reserve, decorum or genteel niceties.

3

Indeed, few of the poems written by female poets are comfortable or comforting, or motherly. Even Barker's poem, *Material*, most obviously concerned with motherhood and expressing love and respect for the poet's mother, maintains a critical stance towards traditional notions of femininity and motherhood, articulating a determination to go forward with a less constricted, gendered identity. As her choice of a non-gendered poetry name suggests, U.A. Fanthorpe's poem is hardly marked at all by gender. Indeed it would be interesting to test in the classroom whether students identify the narrator in the poem as female. If so, it might only suggest that the role of a carer is still often assumed to be a female one.

What else might our Victorian time traveller find strange? Perhaps they'd be struck by how many foreign sounding names there are in the list. Ireland, in particular, contributes a number of poets disproportionate to its population. Heaney is joined here by Irish poets from a similar generation, such as Carson, O'Driscoll, Duhig and Boland, as well as by much younger Irish poets, such as Flynn and Morrissey. Together they make up about a quarter of the selected poems, though we have to acknowledge that we've lumped in Northern Irish poets with those from the Republic. Perhaps our imaginary poet would care to speculate about what it is about the emerald isle that means it produces so many writers of stature and what these poems have in common.

A few decades ago we might reasonably have expected Irish poetry to deal directly or obliquely with issues of nationalism and Catholicism. But, according to Justin Quinn, in the twenty-first century there has been a 'gradual abandonment of the nation as a framework for Irish poetry'.[1] Indeed, in terms of style or subject, is there anything distinctly Irish about the poems in the Forward Anthology? We don't think so. Should we read these poems through the prism of post-colonial theory, in terms of colonising subject and colonised other? It is an option, but not a necessary way of reading the poems. To us, these poems seem to fit Quinn's lyrical description of freeing themselves from the constraints of nationalism like 'butterflies' taking 'flight from museum

---

[1] Justin Quinn, *The Cambridge Introduction to Modern Irish Poetry*, p.1

cases'[2]

Names such as Padel, Agbabi, Nagra and Szirtes signal the increasingly plural, richly cosmopolitan nature of British society and the art we produce. Colloquial and idiomatic though their language often is, generally the poets stick to a loose, demotic form of Standard English. Though a number of the poets employ dialectic words, such as Heaney's use of 'lug' and Duhig's reference to 'muckle sorrow', surprisingly few of these poems are written in one of the many common variants of English. Arguably the syntax of Nagra's poems captures a non-standard English voice.

Though the treatment of themes would be unfamiliar and challenging for our Victorian poet, the topics of many of these poems would be more

 recognisable. Poems such as Armitage's, Motion's or O'Driscoll's about the individual's relationship with the natural world or with the societies within which we live; poems such as Carson's and Burnside's that explore the significance of history and our place within it; poems such as Boyle's or Thorpe's which explore concepts of beauty or love; poems such as Copus' and Dunmore's which examine growing up; poems about place and its importance in shaping our identities, such as Duffy's and Heaney's, and so on. Arguably these are some of the eternal subjects of poetry - the self and others, the self and society, love, death. I expect our Victorian poet might be shocked by all this material reality and the absence of any devotional poetry, the almost entire absence, indeed, of the Christian God. That's not to say, however, that a mysterious or spiritual or mythic or religious dimension is missing for all these poems, just that when it is there it tends to be approached obliquely.

Would our increasingly real-seeming poet be impressed? By the unprudish

---

[2] Ibid, p.204

frankness of lines like 'when sex was fresh', or by the direct shocking violence of 'her throat was cut', or by the throwaway colloquialism of 'knocked back a quarter-pint'? Would he be puzzled or delighted by the diction-busting, ubiquitous references to the bits and bobs of modern culture: 'a handful of bills/ or a giro', 'A-Z street maps', 'chemotherapy', 'genetics', automated telephone services, 'kitschy vases', 'paper tissues', 'the TV in the corner'? Unfortunately we'll never know, of course. But we like to think that poets are, by nature, generous, curious souls, so our fellow is entranced by the extraordinary range of voices, opinions, styles, language, approaches, tones in the **Forward Poems of the Decade** anthology. Our poet is moved and challenged, made to think, made to feel, made to feel frustrated perhaps. And sometimes puzzled. But made too to smile or laugh - by the quietly contemplative and philosophical poems, by the technically agile, dexterous ones, by the spooky ones and the unnerving ones, by the poems that are angry and brave, by those that are nakedly honest and poignantly tenderly quietly intimate. We hope that like you, our poet will be up to the task of properly appreciating these poems and that he'll conclude from studying them that modern poetry must be in vibrant and robust good health!

# Modern poetry published in Britain

To misquote Andrew Marvell a little, had we but space enough and time we would, of course, provide a comprehensive overview of developments in British poetry from Thomas Hardy through to the most recently published work. Unfortunately, or perhaps, fortunately for you, we have neither the space nor time to produce this here. And, to be honest, nor do A-level students or their teachers need a comprehensive literary context for **Poems of the Decade**. Marks in the Edexcel exam, will be rewarded for quality of close reading, for writing and for the strength of the comparison made. There are no marks for context. Hence we have not written short potted biographies for each poet in the following essays. In any case, a little research on the internet will provide this information for the diligent student. If you are curious enough to want a comprehensive treatment of developments in poetry in the twentieth century, we strongly recommend **The Oxford English Literary History, volume 12, Part II**, by Randall Stevenson.

If there are no marks for context, why read this? Because understanding of context is always enriching. An understanding of the literary context deepens appreciation of any text. Context may not determine meanings, but it certainly has a significant effect on them. Consider, for instance, the following sentence, 'the duck is ready to eat'. How does the meaning of this sentence change if we change the context? If the context is a restaurant one meaning is clear. But a different meaning is evinced if the context is a pond. Other meanings entirely would come into play if the sentence were heard in a gangster or spy movie. And so on. So, whether they are officially rewarded through assessment objectives or not, contexts (literary, socio-historical and of reception) are always, always significant.

### Mainstream and the avant-garde
In all forms of art there is a mainstream and an avant-garde. After T. S. Eliot launched **The Waste Land** on an unsuspecting public in the 1920s and the Modernist Movement swept through the arts world, throwing everything up in

the air, a split developed in English poetry that still, arguably, persists to this day. On one side were poets committed to the sort of radical thematic, stylistic and formal experimentalism that Modernism promoted. On the other were poets who considered Modernism to be too radical, excessive and self-obsessed. This second set of poets sought to maintain continuity with earlier, traditional English poetry.

As Peter Howarth writes in **The Cambridge Introduction to Modernist Poetry**, the term Modernism would perhaps better be replaced by Modernisms, such is the diversity of different artistic movements and trends associated with it. Howarth draws a useful parallel with jazz:

'...perhaps the best analogy is to see modernism as an umbrella term: a recognisable genre of music which emerged among various artists who found themselves part of a growing 'movement', rather than being invented singlehandedly at one time or place. Like jazz, it has different but related sub-genres with it (Futurism, Imagism, Objectivism, Surrealism and many others), some intense internal rivalries...and much creative fusion with other art forms.'
3

However, despite the various sub-genres, we can discern certain trends and approaches common to most Modernist texts. For one thing, as the name implies, Modernist texts wanted to be modern. In the new machine age of the early twentieth century previous modes of art seemed suddenly outdated, redundant, unfit to capture a new reality. A new age needed a new literature, one that was leaner, fitter, more angular, more machine-like, more real. If nothing else, Modernist texts share an antagonism for, and rejection of, the values and procedures of the Victorian age.

Modernist painters dumped the traditional single perspective and aesthetics; modernist poets binned the metronome of metre and regular form; modernist composers dispensed with melody and regular time signatures and embraced dissonance; modernist architects replaced bricks with steel and glass.

---

[3] Peter Howarth, *The Cambridge Introduction to Modernist Poetry*, p.4

Hostility to convention was in vogue. Experimentation ruled. The world reeled before the shock of the new.

The father of modern Psychology, Sigmund Freud, was a pervasive influence: Generally interested in the mind and the workings of the subconscious, Modernist texts tend to explore topics traditionally outlawed as taboo. For example, in novels, Modernists rejected traditional, rational models of character formation, developing instead the 'stream of consciousness' to reveal the subconscious drives supposedly governing characters' behaviour.

Relativist in outlook, Modernists wanted to see the world in a different, less fixed way. The subject of their art is broken up and broken down. As the

image of Juan Gris's 1918 painting, *The Guitar*, illustrates, rather than seeing and presenting their subject from a single, fixed perspective, Modernists favoured presenting multiple, even potentially contradictory, points of view. In the novel, for instance, the Victorian preference for God-like omniscient narration gave way to stories related through the less reliable narration of various major and minor characters. Hence, generally Modernism is characterised by a radical collage approach: Incongruous elements are combined, so that structurally and linguistically texts become assemblies of seemingly disparate fragments.

Often drawing on classical literature as a form of ironic intertextual contrast, Modernist works also tend to be self-reflexive - in dialogue with themselves and their own procedures.

9

Modernism was, and still is, challenging. As anyone who has read *The Waste Land* or tried to read Joyce's seminal Modernist novel, **Ulysses,** will know, Modernist texts tend to be rather taxing on the old grey matter. For its original audience, Igor Stravinsky's modernist masterpiece **The Rites of Spring** was so hard to listen to the first audiences broke out in violent riot. Modernist paintings were frequently considered scandalous and banned. Consider, as an example, Picasso's famous painting **Les Demoiselles d'Avignon**, painted in 1907, but not first exhibited until 1916, and a prime example of early Modernism in the visual arts:

Not exactly a conventional depiction of the female nude is it?

In contrast, traditionalist poets eschewed what they considered to be the self-indulgent excesses, elitism, vogue for fragmentation and the brain-bending

difficulties of Modernism. Instead these writers favoured well-crafted, sonorous and coherent poems, poems which aimed to communicate comprehensible meaning to a wide audience. They favoured what might be called the comfort of the old. Focusing on capturing 'the real', antipathetic to anything smacking of redundant Romanticism, illogical mysticism or the foreign fancy avant-gardism of Modernism, these poets championed the traditional craft skills of writing. For them writerly craft and tradition was embodied in the work of the Victorian poet, Thomas Hardy, pictured here.

In his biography of the poet, Ted Hughes, Jonathan Bate usefully outlines developments in twentieth century poetry after Modernism: 'The radical experimentation of T. S. Eliot and Ezra Pound had given way to the political poetry of the 1930's and then in the Forties the passionate rhetoric of Dylan Thomas was a reaction against the cool intellectualism of W. H. Auden. The Movement of the Fifties was, in turn, a reaction against the 'wild loose emotion' of Thomas.' [4]

The Movement poets of the 1950s and 60s gave the traditionalists' emphasis on well-made poems a contemporary, down-to-earth, restrained and peculiarly English spin. These poets often took a detached, ironic role to comment disaffectedly on modern culture and on the experience of the often lone individual within it. Characteristically they combined traditional, regular poetic forms with modern, colloquial English. In doing so they developed a poetic aesthetic that dominated the mainstream of English poetry for many decades. Arguably, indeed, their ideas still have a powerful influence on

---

[4] Jonathan Bate, *Ted Hughes, The Unauthorised Life*, pp. 179-180

contemporary poetry. Philip Larkin is probably the most famous poet associated with The Movement.

In the 1960s other strains kicked hard against this mainstream. Notably the work of Ted Hughes and his wife, Sylvia Plath, and, in America, the rhapsodic style of the Beats and the shocking candour of the Confessional poets. At the start of the decade, the influential critic Al Alvarez produced an anthology called, tellingly, *The New Poetry* in the introduction to which he argued that poetry had to move beyond the restrictions and limitations of what he dubbed the Movement's 'gentility principle'. A champion first of Hughes and later too of Plath, Alvarez demanded that poetry be less buttoned-up, more charged with fierce passion, more extreme, more capable, in fact, of expressing the truth of life in an era containing two world wars, concentration camps, and genocide. Poetry had to up to the task of conveying life in a time haunted by the threat of nuclear obliteration.

Usefully, Plath's poetry embodies a tension between two contrary strains in poetry that are still traceable in the Forward anthology. On the one hand she was influenced by the European symbolist and surrealist poets. Rather than writing directly about their experiences, these poets used the symbolic language of dreams and of myths. Symbolism and the mythic mode can be seen as an attempt to universalise experience, but it also provides some protective cover for a poet. On the other hand, Plath's poetry was shaped by the Confessional style of poetry coming from the  States, particularly associated with the work of Robert Lowell. In contrast to symbolist work, Confessional poets made their own autobiography their chief subject, writing about it in a direct, undisguised style. The courage of Confessional poets lies in the naked exposure of intensely personal details of their often troubled and complex lives. Because of its exploration of taboo subjects, such as extreme emotions, sex, death, addiction, madness and so forth, Confessional poetry was often shocking and controversial. Broadly speaking, the content of Plath's poetry may be nakedly confessional but her treatment applies the veil of the symbolic and surrealist.

Another influential anthology reflecting, but also shaping, the terrain of British poetry was Andrew Motion and Blake Morrison's **Penguin Book of British Writing**, published in 1982. This anthology was notable for its conservative choices (all the poets in Alvarez's anthology were excluded, few female and no black poets were chosen). In the second half of the twentieth century the radical strain in British poetry continued as a counter to this more commercial mainstream. Its stance and perspective was well articulated by Iain Sinclair in the provocative introduction to his anthology of English poetry, which, even in its title sticks a metaphorical two fingers up to The Movement and its followers. First published in 1996, Sinclair's anthology **Conductors of Chaos** can be seen as a rejoinder to Motion and Morrison. Here's a taste of the introduction:

> The work I value is that which seems most remote, alienated, fractured. I don't claim to 'understand' it but I like having it around. The darker it grows outside the window, the worse the noises from the island, the more closely do I attend to the mass of instant-printed pamphlets that pile up around my desk. The very titles are pure adrenalin: *Satyrs and Mephitic Angels, Tense Fodder, Hellhound Memos, Civic Crime, Alien Skies, Harpmest Intermezzi, A Pocket History of the Soul.* You don't need to read them, just handle them: feel the sticky heat creep up through your fingers....Why should they be easy? Why should they not reflect some measure of the complexity of the climate in which they exist? Why should we not be prepared to make an effort, to break sweat, in hope of high return?

Sinclair goes on to offer some interesting advice on how to read any poem, but especially a radical, avant-garde one:

> There's no key, no Masonic password: take the sequence gently, a line at a time. Treat the page as a block, sound it for submerged sonar

effects. Suspend conditioned reflexes...if it comes too sweetly, somebody is trying to sell you something.

Try placing all the set poems in the Forward Anthology on a continuum from, at one end, avant-garde/ radical/ experimental and at the other end mainstream/ traditional/ well-made. Repeat the exercise, only this time arrange the poems by their various constituent elements - form, language, themes. Some poems, might, for instance, be radical in terms of content, but more conventional in form, or vice versa. At the end of this process you should develop a sense of which poem is the most radical and which the most traditional in approach. Which is better, or, indeed, whether one style is better than another, is for you to judge.

What might the ultimate radical avant-garde poetry of today look like? Perhaps it might be a poem that seems to reject all the traditional attributes that make a poem a poem. Or dispense with all the traditional tools, such as imagery. More radical perhaps would be a poet that denied themselves the use of anything other than function words. How about a poem made entirely of conjunctions, prepositions and articles? What might that look like? Or more radically still, perhaps, the most avant-garde poets might dispense with words entirely, constructing poems just from punctuation. How would you go about writing, or worse, analysing such a poem? If this seems too far-fetched, spare a thought for the Cambridge English undergraduates who were set a wordless poem constructed just of brackets, question and exclamation marks to analyse in their finals exam (though, to be fair to the university, they were at least given the title). In this light, reading the Forward anthology poems we've a much easier task.

# Tackling the unseen

If Literature is a jungle, of all the beasts that roam or lurk among its foliage, from the enormous, lumbering Victorian state-of-the-nation novel to the carnivorous revenge tragedy, the most dangerous by far is a small, fast-moving beast, a beast untethered by place or time, a beast that is, in fact invisible. This infamous critter is called, simply, 'the unseen'.

Well, that's sounds all rather alarming. Let's bring the rhetoric down a notch or ten. How should you go about analysing an unseen poem and how can you prepare for this demanding task? In this case, by 'unseen' we don't mean the sort of poem those poor undergraduates had to analyse, i.e. a poem without any words, but a poem you see for the first time in the examination hall.

To start with, we need to make clear that we don't believe there's one universally right method for reading poems. If there were, all the varied types of literary theorists - Feminist, Marxist, postcolonial and so forth – would have to adopt the same working methods. Like the children depicted below, critics

and theorists do not, in fact, all read in the same way. So, it's vital to appreciate that there's no single master key that will unlock all poems. A uniformly applicable method of reading a poem, or of writing about it in an examination, or for coursework, is like the philosopher's stone; it just does not exist. Or as Iain Sinclair puts it, there's no 'Masonic password' that will give you instant access to the locked inner chamber of a poem's most secret meanings.

Having a singular method also makes the foolish assumption that all poems can be analysed in exactly the same way. A mathematician who thinks all maths problems can be solved with one method probably won't get very far, we expect. Instead you need to be flexible. Trust your own trained reading skills. Respond to the key features of the text that is in front of you as you see them. It's no good thinking you will always write your second paragraph on figurative imagery, for instance, because what are you going to do when confronted with a poem entirely devoid of this feature, such as Ciaran O'Driscoll's *Please Hold*? Although all the essays in this book explore fundamental aspects of poetry, such as language, form, themes, effects and so forth, we haven't approached these aspects in a rigid, uniform or mechanical way. Rather our essays are shaped by what we found most engaging about each poem. For some poems this may be the use the poet has made of form. This is likely to be the case if, for instance, the poet has used a traditional form, such as a villanelle. For other poems the striking thing might be imagery; for others still it might be the way the poet orchestrates language to bring out its musical properties.

In terms of critical approach, we'd champion well-informed individual freedom above over-regulated and imposed conformity. Hence, we hope our essays will be varied and interesting and a little bit unpredictable, a bit like the poems themselves. We trust that if you write astutely about how a poet's techniques contribute to the exploration of themes and generation of effects you really won't be going far wrong.

(If you're interested in trying different methods of analysing poems, there is a concise guide in our A-level companion book, *The Art of Writing English Literature essays, for A-level and Beyond*).

To reiterate: Always keep to the fore of your essay the significance and impact of the material you're analysing. Very sophisticated analysis involves exploring how different aspects of the poem work in consort to generate effects. As a painter uses shapes, brush strokes, colours and so forth, or a composer uses chords, notes and time signatures, so a poet has a range of poetic devices at his or her disposal.

Think of a poem as a machine built to remember itself. Your task is to take apart the poem's precision engineering - the various cogs, gears and wheels that make the poem go - and to examine carefully how they operate. If you can also explain how they combine together to generate the poem's ideas and feelings you will, without a shadow of a doubt, achieve top marks.

We believe your essays must express your own thoughts and feelings, informed by the discipline of literary study and by discussion with your teachers and peers. And, that your essays should be expressed in your own emerging critical voice. Finding, refining and then trusting your own critical voice is part of the self-discovery that contributes to making English Literature such a rewarding subject to study at A-level.

Offering quality support material, a safety net, if you like, for your walk on the tightrope of interpretation, we hope the essays offered here will give you the confidence to make it across to the other side. Or to switch metaphors, our essays are designed to provide you with the maps and tools, the essential survival kit in fact, that will help you master this collection of poems and to tame the unseen. In achieving this, you should also achieve great grades in your exams.

# Writing comparative essays

The following is adapted from our discussion of this topic in *The Art of Writing English Literature Essays* course companion book, and is a briefer version, tailored to the Edexcel exam task. Fundamentally comparative essays want you to display not only your ability to intelligently talk about literary texts, but also your ability to make meaningful connections between them. The first starting point is your topic. This must be broad enough to allow substantial thematic overlapping of the texts. However, too little overlap and it will be difficult to connect the texts; too much overlap and your discussion will be lopsided and one-dimensional. In the case of the Edexcel exam, the board will determine the topic they want you to discuss. The exam question will ask you to focus on the methods used by the poets to explore a particular theme. You will also be directed to write specifically on themes, language and imagery as well as other poetic techniques.

One poem from the set text will be specified. You will then have to choose a companion poem. Selecting the right poem for interesting comparison is obviously very important. To think about this visually, you don't want Option A, below, [not enough overlap] or Option B [two much overlap]. You want Option C. This option allows substantial common links to be built between your chosen texts where discussion arises from both fundamental similarities AND differences.

**Option A: too many differences**

**Option B: too many similarities**

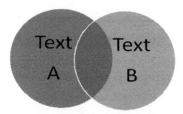

**Option C: suitable number of similarities and differences**

The final option will generate the most interesting discussion as it will allow substantial similarities to emerge as well as differences. The best comparative essays actually find that what seemed like clear similarities become subtle differences and vice versa while still managing to find rock solid similarities to build their foundations on.

How should you structure your comparative essay? Consider the following structures. Which one is best and why?

### Essay Structure #1

1. Introduction
2. Main body paragraph #1 - Text A
3. Main body paragraph #2 - Text A
4. Main body paragraph #3 - Text B
5. Main body paragraph #4 - Text B
6. Conclusion

**Essay Structure #2**

1. Introduction
2. Main body paragraph #1 - Text A
3. Main body paragraph #2 - Text A
4. Main body paragraph #3 - Text B
5. Main body paragraph #4 - Text B
6. Comparison of main body paragraphs #1 & #3 - Text A + B
7. Comparison of main body paragraphs #2 & #4 - Text A + B
8. Conclusion

**Essay Structure #3**

1. Introduction
2. Main body paragraph #1 - Text A + B
3. Main body paragraph #2 - Text A + B
4. Main body paragraph #3 - Text A + B
5. Main body paragraph #4 - Text A+ B
6. Conclusion

We hope you will agree that 3 is the optimum option. Option 1 is the dreaded 'here is everything I know about text A, followed by everything I know by Text B' approach where the examiner has to work out what the connections are between the texts. This will score the lowest AO4 marks. Option 2 is better: There is some attempt to compare the two texts. However, it is a very inefficient way of comparing the two texts. For comparative essay writing the most important thing is to discuss both texts together. This is the most effective and efficient way of achieving your overall aim. Option 3 does this by comparing and contrasting the two texts under common umbrella headings. This naturally encourages comparison. Using comparative discourse markers, such as 'similarly', 'in contrast to', 'conversely' 'likewise' and 'however' also facilitates effective comparison.

When writing about each poem keep the bullet points in mind. Make sure you do not work chronologically through a poem, summarising the content of each stanza. Responses of this sort typically start with 'In the first stanza' and employ discourse markers of time rather than comparison, such as 'after', 'next', 'then' and so forth. Even if your reading is analytical rather than summative your essay should not work through the poem from the opening to the ending. Instead, make sure you write about the ideas explored in both texts (themes), the feelings and effects generated and the techniques the poets utilise to achieve these.

# Writing about language

Poems are paintings as well as windows; we look at them as well as through them. As you know, special attention should be paid to language in poetry because of all the literary art forms poetry, in particular, employs language in a precise, self-conscious and distinctive way. Ideally in poetry, every word should count. Analysis of language falls into a number of different categories:

- By **diction** we mean the vocabulary used in a poem. A poem might be composed from the ordinary language of everyday speech or it might use elaborate, technical or elevated phrasing. Or both. At one time some words and types of words were considered inappropriate for the rarefied field of poetry. The great Irish poet, W. B. Yeats never referred to modern technology in his poetry, there are no cars, or tractors or telephones, because he did not consider such things fitting for poetry. When much later, Philip Larkin used swear words in his otherwise well-mannered verse the effect was deeply shocking. Modern poets have pretty much dispensed with the idea of there being an elevated literary language appropriate for poetry. Hence in the Forward collection you'll find all sorts of modern, everyday language, including some forthright swearing.
- **Grammatically** a poem may use complex or simple sentences (the key to which is the conjunctions); it might employ a wash of adjectives and adverbs, or it may rely extensively on the bare force of nouns and verbs. Picking out and exploring words from specific grammatical classes has the merit of being both incisive and usually illuminating.
- Poets might mix together different types, conventions and registers of language, moving, for example, between formal and informal, spoken and written, modern and archaic, and so forth. Arranging the diction in the poem in terms of **lexico-semantic fields**, by register or by etymology, helps reveal underlying patterns of meaning.
- For almost all poems **imagery** is a crucial aspect of language. Broadly imagery is a synonym for description and can be broken down into two

types, **sensory and figurative**. Sensory imagery means the words and phrases that appeal to our senses, to touch and taste, hearing, smell and sight. Sensory imagery is evocative; it helps to take us into the world of the poem to share the experience being described. Figurative imagery, in particular, is always significant. As we have mentioned, not all poems rely on metaphors and similes; these devices are only part of a poet's box of tricks, but figurative language is always important when it occurs because it compresses multiple meanings into itself. To use a technical term figurative images are polysemic - they contain many meanings. Try writing out the all the meanings contained in a metaphor in a more concise and economical way. Even simple, everyday metaphors compress meaning. If we want to say our teacher is fierce and powerful and that we fear his or her wrath we can more concisely say our teacher is a dragon.

# Writing about patterns of sound

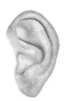

What not to do: Tempting as it may be to spot sonic features of a poem and list these, don't do this. Avoid something along the lines of "The poet uses alliteration here and the rhyme scheme is ABABCDCDEFEFGG." Sometimes, indeed, it may be tempting to set out the poem's whole rhyme scheme like this. Resist the temptation: This sort of identification of features is worth zero marks. Marks in exams are reserved for attempts to link techniques to meanings and to effects.

Probably many of us have been sitting in English lessons listening somewhat sceptically as our English teacher explains the surprisingly specific significance of some seemingly random piece of alliteration in a poem. Something along the lines "The double d sounds here reinforce a sense of invincible strength" or "the harsh repetition of the 't' sounds suggests anger". Through all of our minds at some point may have passed the idea that, in these instances, English teachers appear to be using some sort of Enigma-style secret symbolic decoding machine that reveals how particular patterns of sounds have such particular coded meanings.

And this sort of thing is not all nonsense. Originally deriving from an oral tradition, poems are, of course, written for the ear as much as for the eye, to be heard as much as read. A poem is a soundscape as much as it is a set of meanings. Sounds are, however, difficult to tie to very definite meanings and effects. By way of example, the old BBC Radiophonic workshop, which produced ambient sounds for radio and television programmes, used the same sounds in different contexts, knowing that the audience would perceive them in the appropriate way because of that context. Hence the sound of bacon sizzling, of an audience clapping and of feet walking over gravel were actually recordings of an identical sound. Listeners heard them differently because of the context. So, we may, indeed, be able to spot the repeated 's' sounds in a poem, but whether this creates a hissing sound like a snake or

24

the susurration of the sea will depend on the context within the poem and the ears of the reader. Whether a sound is soft and soothing or harsh and grating is also open to interpretation.

The idea of connecting these sounds to meanings or significance is also a productive one. Your analysis will be most convincing if you use a number of pieces of evidence together. In other words, rather than try to pick out individual examples of sonic effects we recommend you explore the weave or pattern of sounds, the effects these generate and their contribution to feelings and ideas. For example, this might mean examining  how alliteration and assonance are used together to achieve a particular mimetic effect. An example will help demonstrate what we mean.

In *Out of the Bag* Seamus Heaney provides very specific visual imagery, comparing the dark brown interior of an old-fashioned doctor's bag to a skin. Heaney also utilises a number of sonic aspects of language to make the bag vivid:

'Its lined *insides*
(The colour of a spaniel's *inside* lug)'

- alliteration of 'l'
- liquidy 's' sounds running through the line
- assonance of the long, light 'i' sound
- monosyllabic, Anglo-Saxon sounding noun, 'lug' - specific both in terms of part of the dog and, as a dialect word, in terms of place, brings the line to a solid conclusion.

A rich, musical soundworld is constructed. The effect here is clear; to appreciate the full significance you'll need to read our essay on this poem.

# Writing about form & structure

As you know, there are no marks for simply identifying textual features. This holds true for language, sounds and also for form. Consider instead the relationship between a poem's form and its content and effects. Form is not merely decorative or ornamental: A poem's meanings and effects are generated through the interplay of form and content. Broadly speaking the form can either work with or against a poem's content. Conventionally a sonnet, for instance, is about love, whereas a limerick is a comic form. A serious love poem in the form of a limerick would be unusual, as would a sonnet about an old man with a beard.

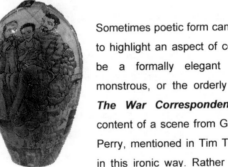

Sometimes poetic form can create an ironic backdrop to highlight an aspect of content. An example would be a formally elegant poem about something monstrous, or the orderly form of Ciaran Carson's **The War Correspondent** containing the chaotic content of a scene from Gallipoli. The artist Grayson Perry, mentioned in Tim Turnbull's poem, uses form in this ironic way. Rather than depicting the sort of picturesque, idealised images we expect of ceramics, Perry's pots and urns depict modern life in bright, vivid colours. The urn pictured, for instance, is entitled **Modern Family** and depicts two gay men with a boy who they have presumably adopted. A thrash metal concert inside a church, a philosophical essay via text message, a fine crystal goblet filled with cherryade would be further examples of an ironic relationships between message and medium, content and context or form.

********

Put a poem before your eyes. Start off taking a panoramic perspective: Think of the forest, not the trees. Perhaps mist over your eyes a bit. Don't even read the words, just look at the poem on the page, like at a painting. Is the poem slight, thin, fat, long, short? What is the relation of whiteness to blackness? Why might the poet have chosen this shape? Does it look regular or irregular? A poem about a long winding river will probably look rather different from one about a small pebble, or should do. Unless form is being employed ironically. Think, for instance, about how Eavan Boland uses form in **Inheritance** to convey a sense of contemplative thought. Now read the poem a couple of times. First time, fast as you can, second time more slowly and carefully. How does the visual layout of the poem relate to what it seems to be about? Does this form support, or create a tension against, the content? Is the form one you can recognise, like a sonnet, or is it, perhaps, free verse? Usually the latter is obvious from irregularity of the stanzas and line lengths.

As Hurley and O'Neill explain in **Poetic Form: An Introduction**, like genre, form sets expectations: 'In choosing form, poets bring into play associations and expectations which they may then satisfy, modify or subvert'. [5] We've already suggested that if we see a poem is a sonnet or a limerick this recognition will set up expectations about the nature of the poem's content. The same thing works on a smaller level; once we have noticed that a poem's first stanza is a quatrain, we expect it to continue in this neat, orderly fashion. If the quatrain's rhyme scheme is xaxa, xbxb, in which only the second and fourth lines rhyme, we reasonably expect that the next stanza will be xcxc. So, if it isn't we need to consider why.

So after taking in the big picture in terms of choice of form now zoom in: Explore the stanza form, lineation, punctuation, the enjambment and caesura. Single line stanzas draw attention to themselves. If they are end-stopped they can suggest isolation, separation. Couplets imply twoness. Stanzas of three lines are called tercets and feature in villanelles and terza rima. On the page, both these forms tend to look rather delicate, especially if separated from each other by the silence of white space. Often balanced through rhyme, quatrains look a bit more robust and sturdy. Cinquains are swollen quatrains in which the last line often seems to throw the stanza out of balance. Some

---

[5] Hurley & O'Neill, *Poetic Form, An Introduction*, p.3

poems, such as O'Driscoll's **Please Hold** squeeze out the space, leave little room for silences by eschewing stanzas almost entirely, presenting themselves as one thick, unbroken block of text. An obvious invitation for analysis.

Focus in on specific examples and on points of transition. For instance, if a poem has four regular quatrains followed by a couplet examine the effect of this change. If we've been ticking along nicely in iambic metre and suddenly trip on a trochee, examine why. Consider regularity. Closed forms of poems, such as sonnets, are highly regular with set rhyme schemes, metre and number of lines. The opposite form is called 'open', the most extreme version of which is free verse. In free verse poems the poet dispenses with any set metre, rhyme scheme or recognisable traditional form. What stops this sort of poetry from being prose chopped up to look like verse? The care of the design on the page. Hence we need to focus here on lineation. Enjambment runs over lines and makes connections, caesura pauses a line and separates words. Lots of enjambment generates a sense of the language running away from the speaker. Lots of caesuras generate a halting, hesitant, choppy movement to lines. Opposites, these devices work in tandem and where they fall is always significant in a good poem.

# Nice to metre...

# A brief guide to metre and rhythm in poetry

Why express yourself in poetry? Why read words dressed up and expressed as a poem? What can you get from poetry that you can't from prose? There are many compelling answers to these questions. Here, though, we're going to concentrate on one aspect of the unique appeal of poetry – the structure of sound in poetry. Whatever our stage of education, we are all already sophisticated at detecting and using structured sound. Try reading the following sentences without any variation whatsoever in how each sound is  emphasised, and they will quickly lose what essential human characteristics they have. The sentences will sound robotic. So, in a sense, we won't be teaching anything new here. It's just that in poetry the structure of sound is carefully unusually crafted and created. It becomes a key part of what a poem is.

We will introduce a few new key technical terms along the way, but the ideas are straightforward. Individual sounds (syllables) are either stressed (emphasised, sounding louder and longer) or unstressed. As well as clustering into words and sentences for meaning, these sounds (syllables) cluster into rhythmic groups or feet, producing the poem's metre, which is the characteristic way its rhythm works.

In some poems the rhythm is very regular and may even have a name, such as iambic pentameter. At the other extreme a poem may have no discernible regularity at all. As we have said, this is called free verse. It is vital to remember that the sound in a good poem is structured so that it combines effectively with the meanings.

For example, take a look at these two lines from Marvell's **To his Coy Mistress**:

'But at my back I alwaies hear
Times winged Chariot hurrying near:'

Forgetting the rhythms for a moment, Marvell is basically saying at this point 'Life is short, Time flies, and it's after us'. Now concentrate on the rhythm of his words.

- In the first line every other syllable is stressed: 'at', 'back', 'al', 'hear'.
- Each syllable before these is unstressed 'But', 'my', 'I', 'aies'.
- This is a regular beat or rhythm which we could write
  ti TUM / ti TUM / ti TUM / ti TUM , with the / separating the feet. ('Feet' is the technical term for metrical units of sound)
- This type of two beat metrical pattern is called **iambic**, and because there are four feet in the line, it is **tetrameter**. So this line is in 'iambic tetrameter'. (Tetra is Greek for four)
- Notice that 'my' and 'I' being unstressed diminishes the speaker, and we are already prepared for what is at his 'back', what he can 'hear' to be bigger than him, since these sounds are stressed.
- On the next line, the iambic rhythm is immediately broken off, since the next line hits us with two consecutive stressed syllables straight off: 'Times' 'wing'. Because a pattern had been established, when it suddenly changes the reader feels it, the words feel crammed together more urgently, the beats of the rhythm are closer, some little parcels of time have gone missing.

A physical rhythmic sensation is created of time slipping away, running out. This subtle sensation is enhanced by the stress-unstress-unstress pattern of words that follow, 'chariot hurrying' (TUM-ti-ti, TUM-ti-ti). So the hurrying sounds underscore the meaning of the words.

# 13 ways of looking at a poem

Though conceived as pre-reading exercises, most of these tasks work just as well for revision.

1. Mash them (1) – mix together lines from two or more poems. The students' task is to untangle the poems from each other.

2. Mash them (2) – the second time round make the task significantly harder. Rather than just mixing whole lines, mash the poems together more thoroughly, words, phrases, images and all, so that unmashing seems impossible. At first sight.

3. Dock the last stanza or few lines from a poem. The students' have to come up with their own endings for the poem. Compare with the poet's version. Or present the poem without its title. Can the students come up with a suitable one?

4. Break a poem into segments. Split the class into groups. Each group work in isolation on their segment and feedback on what they discover. Then their task is to fit the poem and their ideas about it together as a whole.

5. Give the class the first and last stanza of a poem. Their task is to provide the filling. They can choose to attempt the task at beginner level (in prose) or at world class level (in poetry).

6. Add superfluous words to a poem. Start off with obvious interventions, such as the interjection of blatantly alien, noticeable words. Try smuggling 'pineapple', 'bourbon' and 'haberdashers' into any of the poems and see if you can get it past the critical sensors.

7. Repeat the exercise – This time using much less extravagant words. Try to smuggle in a few intensifiers, such as 'really', 'very' and 'so'. Or extra adjectives.

8. Collapse the lineation in a poem and present it as continuous prose. The students' task is to put it back into verse. Discussing the various pros and cons or various possible arrangements – short lines, long lines, irregular lines - can be very productive. Pay particular attention to line breaks and the words that end them. After a whatever-time-you-deem-fit, give the class the pattern of the first stanza. They then have to decide how to arrange the next stanza. Drip feed the rest of the poem to them.

9. Find a way to present the shapes of each poem on the page without the words. The class should work through each poem, two minutes at a time, speculating on what the shape might tell us about the content of the poem. This exercise works especially well as a starter activity. We recommend you use two poems at a time, as the comparison helps students to recognise and appreciate different shapes.

10. Test the thesis that an astute reader can recognise poems by men from those written by women. Give the class one of the poems such as **The Furthest Distance I've Travelled** or **Effects** without the name of the poet. Ask them to identify whether the writer is male or female and to explain their reasons for identifying them as such. Try again with **A Minor Role**, for which you needn't withhold the poet's name.

11. Split the class into groups. Each group should focus their analysis on a different feature of the poem. Start with the less obvious aspects: Group 1 should concentrate on enjambment and caesuras; group 2 on punctuation; group 3 on the metre and rhythm; group 4 on function words – conjunctions, articles, prepositions. 2-5 mins. only. Then swap focus, four times. Share findings.

12. In **Observations on Poetry**, Robert Graves wrote that 'rhymes properly used are the good servants whose presence at the dinner-table gives the guests a sense of opulent security; never awkward or over-clever, they hand the dishes silently and professionally. You can trust them not to interrupt the conversation or allow their personal disagreements to come to the notice of the guests; but some of them are getting very old for their work'. Explore the poets' use of rhyme in the light of Graves' comment. Are the rhymes ostentatiously original or old hat? Do they stick out of the poem or are they neatly tucked in? Are they dutiful servants of meaning or noisy disrupters of the peace?

13. The Romantic poet, John Keats, claimed that 'we hate poetry that has a palpable design upon us – and if we do not agree seems to put its hand its breeches pock'. Apply his comment to this selection of poems. Do any seem to have a 'palpable design' on the reader? If so, how does the poem want us to respond?

# Forward Poems of the Decade

*(A poem) begins in delight, it inclines to the impulse, it assumes direction with the first line laid down, it runs a course of lucky events, and ends in a clarification – not necessarily a great clarification, such as sects and cults are founded on, but in a momentary stay against confusion. It has denouement. It has an outcome that though unforeseen was predestined from the first image of the original mood.*

**Robert Frost**

# Leontia Flynn, *the furthest distance I've travelled*

A hundred years ago Russian Formalist critics developed the theory of *ostranenie,* or defamiliarisation as it is known in English. These critics argued that in the modern age human responses become automated, deadened and unresponsive to the overly familiar world around us. It is the role of art to make us see the world anew by presenting it to us from an unusual angle. As the marvellously names Formalist critic Victor Shklovsky put it, 'Habitualization devours works, clothes, furniture, one's wife, and fear of war... art exists that one may recover the sensation of life...' [6]. On a smaller literary scale, metaphor is also a way of seeing something afresh through the comparison with something unexpectedly similar.

They say that travel broadens the mind. Encountering different cultures, landscapes, people, language, food and so forth furnishes us with more possibilities and options for how to live our lives. Travel can also do something analogous to defamiliarisation and to metaphor: Stepping out of our usual lives and cultures, experiencing something different, helps us to reflect back on our life and culture in a comparative light. If you've holidayed somewhere hot and arid in the summer, for instance, I expect on your return you appreciated afresh the greenness and lushness of the English landscape.

---

[6] Quoted in Lodge, *The Art of Fiction*, p.53

(You might also have noticed the rain, but then it's pretty hard to forget that.) What is homesickness if not a realisation of one's love for a place we normally take for granted?

The first three breezy stanzas of Flynn's poem express the sort of wanderlust that drives those lucky enough to have gap years abroad. That this is a common feeling is expressed immediately, 'like many folk'. The informal, relaxed register suits the context of backpacking to far-flung places. The jaunty rhythm and decisive, positive vibe carry through these stanzas. For example, the emphatic series of monosyllables in 'I thought: Yes. This is how/ to live'. Enjambment between lines and over stanza breaks adds to the poem's energetic forward momentum. Palpable excitement is in the air:

- exotic place names are mentioned, making the idea of travelling concrete - 'the Sherpa pass'; 'Krakow'; 'Zagreb'; 'Siberian' all tumble out in a breathless list
- three figures of speech are used in quick succession - the spine 'like a meridian', the airport like a 'cell', the idea clear as a 'tannoy'
- the poet is inspired into clever paradox - finding herself ('destiny') in losing herself ('anonymity').
- most of the lines are also short and zippy, as one idea leads quickly on to the next. There are only two full stops, one of which is internal to a line, so that when we arrive at the second, after 'destiny', it is the first time really that the poem has paused to catch its breath.

What's the effect of the irregular within the regular form?
Though the poem is arranged in quatrains, the first three stanzas are strikingly irregular. There are some very long and some very short lines, the shortest, rather audaciously, is just the tail-end fragment of a word, '-mity'. There is an unusual rhyme scheme too, with the first two lines forming a couplet in each of the first two stanzas, before this pattern reverses in the third. The change in the pattern creates sonically a sense of completion of this first section of the poem. It's as if the youthful exuberance to travel expressed by the words is

barely contained by the poem's form, as if the stanzas and their good lieutenants the punctuation are straining to keep the zestfulness in order. What do you make of the striking use of 'mity' as a line? Does it suggest an exuberant devil-may-careness in the narrator, breaking words and rules wherever she fancies? Or might the forcing of the word into the rhyme pattern by breaking it in two signal something running counter to the poem's overt enthusiasm? The latter idea could be supported by the vague, rather wishy-washiness of the phrase 'some kind of destiny'. As we come to the end of the third stanza there are hints that despite her apparent enthusiasm, the poet is having reservations. Or perhaps between the end of stanza three and the opening of four a significant period of time has flashed by and the speaker is now older and wiser. Such a reading suggests another way of interpreting the opening stanzas with a kind of double perspective.

The retrospective nature of the narration ['when first I saddled'] indicates that the poem is written at a later stage looking back at how the narrator used to feel about travel. Hence it combines the innocent enthusiasm they felt at the

time with a later, more experienced, reflective self-awareness. It is the latter perspective we pick up as a tonal counter strain to the surface enthusiasm.

Slight subtextual unease prepares us subtly for the shift in the fourth stanza. We learn that despite all her energetic zeal the poet either hasn't set off on amazing adventures or that her days of backpacking are now over. The pace of the poem slows, lines lengthen, the sense of forward momentum dissipates. Stanzas four and five are structured around contrast. Exotic locations the poet could have travelled to, 'Larium', 'Western Union', 'Madison', 'Milwaukee' are evoked only to make the contrast with reality of being in a post office more poignant. And, instead of doing exciting, extraordinary things in exciting, extraordinary places, such as catching an American 'Greyhound' bus, the poet is doing crushingly boring, everyday, ordinary chores - paying 'bills' or a 'giro', doing her 'laundry'. Whereas at the start of the poem, the speaker had seemed master of her destiny, even if her language appeared in constant danger of running away from her, she does not seem to know now how she arrived at this particular impasse. The sense of deflation is nicely captured in a neatly turned couplet:

**'...I am less likely/ to be catching a Greyhound from Madison to Milwaukee/ than to be doing some overdue laundry'**

Though, as we recognised in the first three stanzas there seems to be a counter strain running against the overt meaning of the words. Here, for example, there's a bounciness to the rhythm, reinforced by a run of 'e' rhymes, from 'likely' through to 'beyond me'. Perhaps things are not so bad after all. Again this undercurrent prepares us nicely for the turnaround that will come at the end of the poem.

Quizzically, the poet suggests some possible explanations for a seemingly disappointing turn of events - 'whether' it was x reason or y. Yet 'why' she is where she is really 'beyond' her understanding. It appears she has ended up somewhere unexciting without making any definite choice to be there, a feeling not uncommon to most of us at some points in our lives. When we are young life can seem full of endless opportunities. As we get older, generally speaking, our life choices become more constrained.

One word in the poem is given a line to itself. Perhaps it is the single, most important word in **The Furthest Distance I've Travelled**: 'However'. This is the hinge word on which the whole poem turns.

Can you think of anything less romantic, exotic, thrilling or adventurous than washing a pair of someone else's old pants? I'm struggling to. In the introduction to this book we mentioned the idea of literary language and diction appropriate to the rarefied sphere of poetry. I'd wager as a noun the word 'pants' hadn't been used in any poem until at least the second half of the twentieth century. Only 'y-fronts' could beat in it in a competition for least poetic word. 'Sports sock' might run it close. Anyhow, more than enough about unpoetic pants and socks. The list of places in the opening stanzas is replaced now with a matching list of everyday 'throwaway' ephemera, the ordinary junk we take no notice of, usually, stuff we find in back pockets or down the backs of sofas. Small stuff too, things we easily discard. Flynn uses a simple, but powerful metaphor to flip over our perceptions. In the final two stanzas the lines lengthen as the poem moves into more ruminative, reflective mode. A sense of order and balance is generated by the movement into a repeated, regular rhyme scheme and more even line length. Flynn implies that habit can make us take the people around us for granted. We should see them, she suggests, as being like the countries or continents. Poignantly the poet conveys the importance of valuing our interactions with other people, embedded in these ordinary objects. For this throwaway stuff has value, it is 'what survives/ of holidaying briefly, in other people's 'lives'.

Are you convinced? Is she right? Do you admire her stoicism? Or is the end of the poem an unconvincing rationalisation of the decisions made, or not made? At first the metaphor of holidaying in other people's lives seems apt. But what if your holidays do not feature the adventure of back-packing, but comprise lounging on a beach soaking up the sun?

## Crunching

Crunching a poem is a quick and interesting way of reducing the text to its most significant words. Only one word is chosen per line of the poem. I recommend you have a go at completing this task on your own at first and then compare your crunching with your peers. Through discussion, see if you can come to an agreed class crunched version. Then compare your version to mine.

Of course, the crunching process can be usefully repeated all the way down to the most important few words, or even a single word, in a poem. And it can be easily adapted: Crunching the best lines, or images, crunching through picking out all the nouns or adjectives or verbs, and so forth.

**The Furthest Distance... crunched:**

**RUCKSACK – BACK – SPINE – MERIDIAN – YES – BETWEEN – ZAGREB – AIRPORTS – CLEAR – RESTLESSNESS – DESTINY – WHETHER – THREATS – NOT – LITHUANIAN – BILLS – GIRO – HOLDALL – GREYHOUND – LAUNDRY – BEYOND – HOWEVER – ROUTINE – PANTS – STOWAWAY – FLOWER – KNOW – VALENTINES – TRAVELLED – PEOPLE – LIVES**

**A further crunch...**

**RUCKSACK – RESTLESSNESS – DESTINY – THREATS – LAUNDRY – PANTS – PEOPLE - LIVES**

With its emphasis on the value of human relationships, **_The Furthest Distance..._** could be compared to many of the other poems in the anthology. **_A Minor Role_** springs to mind because of its similar championing of the ordinary and seemingly significant. **_Material_** also shares the use of something seemingly insignificant to reveal significance. The innocence/ experience theme and idea of growing up connects it to **_To My Nine-Year-Old Self_**, while the wry, knowing and winningly self-deprecating narrative voice might make an interesting comparison to Armitage's **_Chainsaw_** poem.

# Roderick Ford, *Giuseppe*

**1**

Roderick Ford is a Welsh poet who spent much of his youth living in locations as disparate as the UK, Australia, and Africa. Whilst he was a young adult, in the 1970s, he received what he described as 'inappropriate' treatment for Asperger's Syndrome, which wasn't diagnosed until much later; he spent much of his time under the influence of heavy tranquilisers and started writing poetry when his medication was stopped.

**Giuseppe** comes from his poetry collection **The Shoreline of Falling** (2005). Ford's work frequently explores the isolating effects of autism; the image of the solitary and voiceless figure is one that Ford revisits. In particular, the liminal existence of the mermaid - half human, and half fish - depicts that fragile membrane between social interaction and isolation that is the hallmark of an autistic existence. This is also shown elsewhere in the collection; in *Lay my Corpse* the human body is described as being consumed by nature, and its voice replaced by the wordless *'conversations of the laughing dead'*.

One of the haunting tensions throughout Ford's work is the contradiction of using words to depict voicelessness. In his poem *Miss Johnson*, the title character never speaks; 'she slept on a cushion in an old wicker basket / and used a lace hankie to cover herself'. In *Giuseppe*, the mermaid only 'screamed like a woman in terrible fear', because 'she was only a fish, and fish can't speak'. This struggle to be heard is challenged by the lucidity of his writing, showing how a poet can use words to distil and piece together an otherwise murky and confusing reality.

## 2

### Using biography

When you read a poem, sometimes it is easy to pinpoint parts of the writing that you think directly link to another piece of information you might know about the poet's life. Do you think it is important to know about the poet's personal background to write most effectively about his or her work?

In this way, *Giuseppe* presents us with an interesting dilemma. We know that Ford is diagnosed as being on the autistic spectrum; people with autism or Asperger's find it difficult to socialise and communicate in the same way that people without these conditions do. Therefore, is the central character of the mermaid in this poem - and her inability to speak - meant to represent the pain of struggling to communicate in the same way that everyone else does? If this is the case, we could, perhaps, look at the poem as being in the 'confessional' genre - a movement of poetry that emerged in the USA in the late 1950s. As we mentioned in the introduction to this book, confessional poetry explores personal experience directly, often delving into and exposing trauma and the inner, private self.

Maybe Ford, in this poem, is expressing what it is like to be spoken for by others - the frustration and anger of not being able to get involved with other people in quite the same way that everyone seems to. However, there are always problems with using a strictly biographical reading, and in any case there are no marks for referring to biographical context in the Edexcel marking scheme. Whilst this is important for your own understanding of the poem, the mark scheme wants you to be able to investigate the 'nuts and bolts' of the text, for which context can inform reading - but only after you have read it and taken it apart first.

Biography might be significant, but all poetry should be judged by its internal qualities of imagery, structure and language. Using these guidelines, another reading of the poem becomes clear; Ford takes his own experience of having Asperger's Syndrome and combines it with the image of the violated female body to suggest many different possible things - for example, that to take away a woman's voice, or to speak over her, is an act of violence.

## 3
### How can we interpret the imagery in this poem?

Anyone who has read *Captain Corelli's Mandolin* (Louis de Bernières, 1994) might well recognise the imagery of the Mediterranean setting of WWII – 'where the bougainvillea grows so well', by 'the dry and dusty ground'. Here the image of the lushness of nature springing after the sterility of war and death is one of hope, of renewal after terrible suffering. Important images that arise in the poem form an overall conceit (an extended metaphor used throughout a poem), in this case, the theme of being silenced by violence during wartime.

The first is the allusion to the Holocaust, an allusion which runs throughout. This is expressed through references to human experimentation:

- 'when they took a ripe golden roe /from her side, the doctor said /this was proof she was just a fish'
- the taking of wedding rings from the corpses of Jews – 'someone tried to take her wedding ring'
- and the rationale that those who were 'simple' (or what Himmler called 'undesirable') deserved to be removed from society, 'butchered on the dry and dusty ground'.

This leads onto another important theme, that of violence towards women. A feminist reading of this poem would underline the narrative, as shown here, of the treatment of women as an

43

oppressed group. Presented as a sort of monster, a 'mermaid', through the poem's male perspective, the female character is thus made unfamiliar, non-human and 'other'. And this 'othering', coupled with her lack of a voice, frees the male characters to treat the female with savage, cannibalistic violence. The female character's horrific death is a compact analogy of the kind of sexual violence and torture used against women in times of war, which functions as an enforced imprinting of one party's, or tribe's, ethnicity, onto the women of the other side. Through forced reproduction, this means that one race gains prevalence and biological power over another; exactly the goal of the Holocaust in seeking to imprint a 'right' ethnicity and to destroy those whom they saw as 'sub-human'. Through making her a fantastical creature, Ford also asks us to find the familiar in the strange and otherworldly. Have a look at the poem again and see who you think are the more powerful or monstrous people here.

Is it the humans, or the mermaid?

This is another way in which the overarching theme of silence is achieved, which again would sit with a feminist criticism of the text. The mermaid, just as sub-human as other socially oppressed groups, can only make noises within the parameters of what is already stereotypically 'female'. Hence she 'screams like a woman in terrible fear'. Her way of expressing herself is reduced to visceral, hysterical sounds, the repeated brash vowel sounds of 'e' and 'I'- 'she', 'fish', 'fish', 'screamed', 'terrible' and 'fear'- supporting this. The middle ground, or 'liminality', between being fish and human is an analogy for women in general, who historically have been seen as defined in relation to to their bodies (the word 'hysteria' comes from the Latin *hystera* for 'womb') and more grounded in 'animal' instincts than men. Though she is called a 'mermaid' and has 'golden roe' taken from her side, the weight of details imply the victim was a real woman:

- 'She was so simple'
- 'One of her hands'
- 'Her throat was cut'

- 'She screamed'
- 'Wedding ring'.

The female character is literally 'butchered', 'cooked and fed to the troops' who have been 'starved'. Her offspring are removed in the strange fashion of a caesarean section, the 'ripe golden roe' coming from her side just as the blood comes from the side of Christ, or Eve from the side of Adam. However, the image here is not redemptive or generative; it ends in death and sterility. Ford uses the many different  treatments of the woman's body to explore the different ways in which we can be physically silenced.

## 4
### Form and structure

Throughout the poem, metre and form are used to underline a general feeling of unrest and unease. For example, the first stanza is filled with irregular lines, the beginning often 'tripping' over a few syllables to get to the first stressed one (stressed beats are underlined): 'in the courtyard behind the aquarium'. However, the two lines that are perfectly in even metre are:

**'the only captive mermaid in the world / was butchered on the dry and dusty ground'**

The first line, built evenly and smoothly evokes beauty, yet quickly moves onto the finality of 'butchered' and the awkwardly jilting 'doctor, a fishmonger, and certain others'.

There are three monosyllabic lines: 'While her throat was cut'; 'and the ring stayed put' and 'or which I thank God'. The last one ends the whole poem with a distressing, emphatic finality, although the 'thank God' could, of course, indicate that the uncle feels shame, therefore making it less distressing. The poem starts and ends with the characters of Uncle Giuseppe and God respectively, the latter of whom is remarkably absent in the rest of the poem. The fact that 'the priest... held one of her hands / while her throat was cut' suggests an image of a hospital chaplain, but also, arguably, of the priest as witness to a martyrdom; either way, Ford goes to no efforts to make him seem 'godly' or pious. The sudden turn towards God at the end of the poem adds a new dimension. If the poet hadn't written the last line, the reader would be forced to judge the actions of the characters in relation to each other, and to their setting. By inserting God into the structure at the very end, the narrator implies that there is a different system of morality by which these characters should be judged.

## 5

### Chinese whispers?

Another important aspect to note is the narrative voice. Ford does not use his narrator as a 'fly-on-the-wall' figure, in the middle of the action and developing along with the events of the poem. Instead, the whole scenario is talked about as being far in the past. Like an archaeological dig, little bits of information are uncovered for the reader to piece together a version of events. In fact, the reader is actually hearing this improbable story third-hand as it comes from the uncle, to the nephew (narrator), to the reader. The effect of these 'chinese whispers' is not only to remove the story further from us, but also to emphasise the fantastical nature of the characters - the very issue of whether or not we can ever receive an unbiased version of historical events becomes important. It is clear that the mermaid's vulnerability is something that brings sorrow and discomfort to both the narrator and the other characters. However, it is not written in the strict form of an elegy, which the Greeks structured as having an opening lament, followed by praise and admiration, then a consoling finish. Do you think the poem has any consoling effect for the reader- is it supposed to have an unsettled ending? Does the form allow for there to be anything other than incomplete snapshots of people, times and places?

The fact that the bougainvillea grows so well suggests growth and redemption

46

from death and sterility, relating to the re-birth of individuals, communities and countries after the World Wars. However, the involvement of both medical and religious authorities, specifically not the armed forces on the front line, implies that every person, and all parts of society, could be seen as implicit in wartime violence.

*Giuseppe* crunched:

**UNCLE – SICILY – COURTYARD – MERMAID – BUTCHERED – PRIEST – THROAT – CUT – SCREAMED – FISH – ROE – BURIAL – WEDDING RING – COOKED – FED – GOD**

The poem explores the images of violence and consumption, and as such could be compared to many of poems in the anthology. *Eat Me* also makes the connection between the female body and food, in a more visceral and graphic way. *Effects* looks at the physical legacy of dying, a useful poem if you want to explore in a deeper way the relationship between the dead and those who are left behind. *Gallipoli* looks at war but has a much more over-arching narrative - <u>*Giuseppe*</u> zooms in on one event and could therefore make a nice comparison. Finally, *The Lammas Hireling* also features a fantastical creature and also explores human mistrust and violence towards an unfamiliar 'other'.

# Seamus Heaney, *out of the bag*

Fatefully dubbed the greatest Irish poet since W. B. Yeats, Seamus Heaney (1939-2013) was a Nobel Prize winning writer who was probably the most famous poet of his generation. Dealing with growing up in a rural home, Heaney's early poems were characterised by the intense, onomatopoeic physicality of their language. The disturbing and challenging poems in his 1975 collection **North** shifted attention away from the formation of self to the turbulent political times in which Heaney lived and, in particular, The Troubles. After winning the Nobel Prize for literature in 1995, Heaney's poetic focus and mode shifted again, this time into something more lyrical and celebratory, into what the poet himself called a poetry concerned with 'crediting marvels'. No doubt the Good Friday Agreement and the progress made by the Northern Ireland peace process contributed to the sense of release and the lifting of a weight from Heaney's poetry.

**Out of the Bag** comes from Heaney's elegiac 2001 collection **Electric Light**. Described on its dust jacket as a book about 'origins...the places where things start from, the ground of understanding', *Electric Light* depicts Heaney's wide-ranging travels over the maps of his memory. Places such as his family home in Ireland, ancient Greece and the violent fenland world of *Beowulf*, which Heaney had recently translated are peopled with literary tutelary spirits, such as Virgil and Dante, as well as the ghosts of recently deceased fellow writers and friends, such as Ted Hughes and Joseph Brodsky.

In **The Loose Box** from this collection Heaney quotes an earlier Irish poet, Patrick Kavanagh, a major influence on him, on the importance of place and of the effect of writing about it; 'the main thing is/ an inner restitution, a purchase come by/ pacing it in words that you feel/ you've found your feet in what 'surefooted' means/ and in the ground of your understanding'. In another poem, **Perch**, Heaney writes about how the fish within a river is 'on hold/ in the everything flows and steady go of the world'. Like other poems in *Electric Light, Out of the Bag,* is characterised by tensions between fluidity and solidity, fragmentation and interconnection, fear as well as joy. In the poem Heaney seeks to hold on to and hold together disparate pieces of the past, not least in order to make sense of the present.

## 2
## Cohesion and coherence
The term cohesion refers to the way texts are stuck together by shared features. A text is cohesive when its constituent elements link through some form of repetition. Coherence refers to cohesion that makes sense, where ideas link to other ideas in a logical and followable sequence. Hence a text can be cohesive, but not coherent, but it cannot be coherent without being cohesive. At first, it seems thay *Out of the Bag* is only cohesive; a collection of disparate memories is forced together through a shared tercet form and a mesh of language. Notice, for example, the repetition of similar words, sometimes unusually close together, such as 'disappear' and 'reappear' in the first stanza, 'insides' and 'inside' in the second, 'came' and 'come' in the fifth. At other times, similar words build linguistic bridges spanning time and place, linking the poem's various narratives. Hence 'came' and 'disappear' at the start of the poem are echoed in the fourth section; 'precincts' in the third also crops up in the fourth and the key word 'incubation' appears both in the second and last sections. Cohesion creates a holding on, a holding together. Only through a closer reading does it become evident that despite its tendency towards fragmentation the poem is also, in fact, coherent.

## 3
## The sublime
What are your own sources of creativity and imaginative inspiration?
From where, from what and from whom do your best ideas come?

These questions lie at the heart of *Out of Bag's* meditation on origins and the mystery of creativity.

Heaney acknowledged his literary debt to the Romantic poets and, in particular, to William Wordsworth, using the following lines from Wordsworth's *The Prelude* in his collection *North*:

**'Fair seedtime had my soul, and I grew up**
**Fostered alike by beauty and by fear.'**

The painting on the left, by Caspar David Friedrich, is called *Wanderer Above the Sea Fog* and expressed the Romantic conceptualisation of the sublime. For the Romantics, inspiration springs from an individual artist's encounters with lofty, awesome, natural experiences. For the Romantics the sublime had a double aspect, containing beauty, but also terror, both, or either, of which could fire the creative imagination. We can see traces of their thinking about the positive dimension of terror in our modern usage of *terrific* as a positive term. In contrast, horror, which the Romantics believed shrinks rather than expands the soul, has no such positive cognate.

Heaney's poem finds inspiration in memories of childhood, the love of his mother, in the classical past, in the wisdom of other writers, in remembered beauty. But also in the child's terror of the Doctor and in the adult Heaney's fear of aging and illness.

**4**
**The doctor**
As Heaney's poem is arranged in four interconnected parts, it seems simplest

to deal with each part in turn before considering the overall effect of them together. Part one is a meditation on the mystery of origins narrated from a small child's perspective. Heaney's characteristic close concentration on a specific object to reveal the whole is evident in his focus on the doctor's bag. Alongside the very specific visual imagery, comparing the bag's interior colour to that of a dog's, Heaney utilises other aspects of language to bring the memory to vivid life:

'Its lined *insides*
(The colour of a spaniel's *inside* lug)'

Alliteration of 'l' and liquidy 's' sounds run through the line, supported by assonance of the light 'i' sound. The solidly monosyllabic, Anglo-Saxon sounding noun, 'lug', is specific both in terms of part of the dog and, as a dialect word, in terms of place. Heaney fans may also recognise the word from his most famous early poem *Digging*, so that the word forges an intertextual chain back to beginning of the poet's oeuvre.

As we commented on earlier, words are repeated with slight variations in a marked and insistent fashion. As well as 'inside', other words are repeated at least twice - 'spaniel', 'colour', 'bag', 'wind', 'lined'. Consecutive words rhyme in 'nosy' and rosy' and phrases echo sonically each other, such as 'saved for him' and 'savoured by him'. Tactile imagery - 'soft hands', 'satin', 'lukewarm' and the lovely 'sud-luscious' - combines with visual - 'gleam' and 'highlights' - and the olfactory - 'a whiff of disinfectant' to generate an intimate sense of physical reality.

Until three quarters of the way through part one, the doctor is presented in a similar way to the other various masters of their craft who appear regularly in Heaney's work. To the child the doctor is a powerful, commanding and compelling presence, 'like a hypnotist' casting a spell of concentration. Or a magician who performs miraculous tricks, making objects appear and disappear, the coup de theatre of which, of course, is the conjuring of a baby. The only hint of the terror to come is the ominous reference to his exit as 'darken(ing) the door'.

When the doctor catches the child's eye in his own glacial gaze, Heaney's

imagination takes flight. In a startling metaphor the eyes are transformed into 'peep holes' to a 'locked room'. Traditionally eyes are considered the windows to the soul, implying that this locked room is the doctor's soul. The poem's perspective stares through the child's terrified eyes at this place of forbidden knowledge. We witness a scene from a horror film; some sort of perverse dissecting or torture chamber where human body parts hang, neatly, on 'steel hooks', like pieces of meat, and blood 'dreeps in the sawdust'. Fantasy and reality fuse in the unsettling image of the rosebud the Doctor wears, as if a secret badge of monstrosity, resembling a child's 'cock'.

## 5

### Academia

At first part two seems entirely unrelated. Like a massive cross-cut in a film, the scene jumps across space and time, from Heaney's childhood home in Ireland and his wide-eyed, boyish perspective, to the theatre at Epidaurus in Greece (shown in the photograph below) many years later. Linguistically the poem now shifts dramatically too, into the learned discourse of a literary academic.

This academic discourse is signalled from the outset by the switch into Latin, by the references to influential intellectuals (who the reader is assumed to know), by the reference to the Ancient Greek, Asclepius, and the school-teacherly parenthetical explanatory note: '(called *asclepions*)'. Google Peter Levi and you'll discover he was an Oxford professor of poetry. Graves refers to the influential poet and expert on Greek myths, Robert Graves, and Asclepius was an ancient Greek god of medicine. Asclepius's daughter, Hygia, was a goddess of health. Clearly we have moved from the home to the academy.

The nature of the discussion of how a theatre is like a hospital, art like medicine and theatre like religious ritual is also more self-consciously elevated, philosophical and reflective. The repetition of the word 'doctor' in 'doctus' links parts one and two cohesively and we come to understand that both sections are concerned with the creation of life. The birth of a human child in part one is replaced by the birth of creative art. The process of creation here is made more explicit:

ritual ➔ altered state of consciousness (here sleep) ➔ epiphany or revelation ➔ meeting the god (moment of creation)

Seamus Heaney rarely used ellipsis in his poetry, so the fact that he employs this device twice in the same poem is significant. The meeting with 'the god...' is followed by another memory, this time only a brief snatch of being part of a procession. It is unclear if this memory is the result of the meeting of not. Memory gives way to memory in quickening succession as narrative is enfolded within narrative. The cohesive link is the change of consciousness signalled by 'nearly fainted'. The poem becomes disorientating, giddily close to fragmenting, almost incoherent. It is not clear, for example, where Heaney is when he bends to pull some grass. And within this memory is folded another altered state of consciousness in the form of a hallucination that loops the narrative back to Doctor Kerlin and Heaney's childhood.

53

Through this vision, the doctor is presented here as an awesome Zeus-like creator figure, fashioning human beings with his 'large', 'big' hands and miraculously bringing them 'swimming' to life. After the intensity of this revelation and creation, like after the meeting with a god, the poet is left 'blinded with sweat/ blinking and shaky'. In classical literature the wind is associated with animation and the forces of creativity. It is therefore entirely fitting that post-creative crisis the light is 'windless'.

Part three is linked through the reference to 'bits of grass' and to illnesses that are perhaps beyond the restitutive and curative powers of poetry. Again place and time are uncertain and slippery. Presumably, for instance, the posting off of the grass occurred at a later time. As if shaken by his experiences, the poet wants 'nothing more' than to rest, 'to lie down' and to be visited by the goddess of health. Significantly, Hygia is associated by Heaney with illumination and vision - she is the 'very eye of the day', she brings clarity and she is a 'haven of light'. Notice how her special status is indicated by the poem's language lifting off into metaphor.

Whereas the impact of revelation of the male deity was disturbing and frightening, the female deity is imagined as benign and soothing. Whereas the poet was 'blinded' after the first revelation, the goddess and his mother bring 'vision'. The stark contrast is underscored by the reference to doors. Heaney's second collection of poems was titled **Door into the Dark** and in it Heaney used the door as a symbol for a gateway into the unknown. Where Dr Kerlin darkened the door, implying a blocking of perception and access, Hygia is an 'undarkening door', a curative gateway of, and to, light. Perhaps the female deity is the beautiful aspect of the sublime, the flip side of the terrible aspect represented by the Doctor.

## 6

### Home again

We circle back to Heaney's childhood and his home in section four. In memory time can curve, move forwards and backwards, fold in on itself. Linguistically this looping is signalled by the verb 'came' whose simplicity hides the mysteries of creation. The language here drops down to the ordinary and conversational, suitable for an intimate interior, domestic scene with mother and child. Once again repetitive patterns of diction are evident: 'I stand alone' – 'standing'; 'again and again'; 'peering, appearing'. Words from earlier in the poem reappear, most significantly 'doctor', 'precinct', 'asleep' and 'incubating'.

In a later poem from *Electric Light* Heaney celebrates a bridge for its 'holding action'. It is, Heaney, suggests 'strain' and 'tension' that actually holds the bridge 'steady' and makes it 'strong'. In *Out of the Bag* the poet performs this holding action, connecting memories, stories and ideas together, taking the strain of keeping whole this large narrative arc in place, making the poem strong, he hopes, through the balancing of its internal tensions.

Time shifts again. Recalling the opening lines of T.S. Eliot's **Four Quartets** ('Time present and time past/ Are both perhaps present in time future /And time future contained in time past') the poem switches into the present tense, an eternal now of memory. Heaney had written a series of loving, tender poems to his mother in a series called Glanmore sonnets, so the end of the poem is a return in another intertextual sense too.

Revealed is a tender, quiet, domestic scene. The poet '(with) standing the passage of time' so that this memory seems 'pure reality' - things are happening 'for real' and he is alone with his mother who is 'asleep'. As he had done as a thurifer (a senior altar server carrying the incense) the small boy acts as willing helper, here in this more intimate, personal creative process, allowed access into a a 'precinct of vision' through his mother's smile. But her final gentle words to him continue to obscure the process of creation and underplay her own central role in it. Significantly it is the male doctor she credits for the creation of the baby.

**7**

Why the characteristic doubling of language in the poem? To me the answer lies in the concept of the sublime and, in particular, its double aspect of beauty and terror. The poem is a rumination on origins and creativity that sets an apparently potent and disturbing male form against a gentler, but actually more powerful and generative female one.

What of the form of the poem? Why tercets?

Generally Heaney's early poems are characterised by his use of large blocks, almost slabs of stanzas. Tercets are less monumental, more delicate, sparer and leaner forms. Dante's *The Divine Comedy* was a key influence on Heaney and he seems to have picked up the tercet form from the great Italian writer. However, Dante's tercets are linked one to another in a continuous chain, forged through a strict rhyme scheme called terza rima. Eschewing rhyme and unmetred, Heaney's tercets are much looser constructions. Thus a tension runs through the poem, a strain between loosening irregularity and solidifying regularity: The consistent use of tercets helps unify the disparate parts of a poem that at times veers close to breaking into fragments.

As this is a long, complex poem, I'm not going to take a word from every line. Here's the poem crunched, section by section:

CAME – DISAPPEAR – REAPPEAR – HANDS – INSIDES – LUG – EMPTY – HYPNOTIST – WIND – DARKEN – KEEL – CAME – ALSO – AGAIN – GLEAM – SATIN – WATER – SUD-LUSCIOUS – SAVOURED – TOWELLED – HELD – SQUIRED – EYES – HYPERBOREAN – LOCKED – SWABBED – HOOKS – BLOOD – PARTS – STRUNG – COCK – BUTTONHOLE

POETA – SANCTUARIES – SHRINES – CURE – POETRY – I – SANATORIUM – INCUBATION – RITUAL – GOD – GROGGY – PROCESSION – FAINTED – HALLUCINATED – DOCTOR – INDEX – LAVED – MIRACULUM – BITS – HANDS – BLINDED – WINDLESS –

CHEMOTHERAPY – COME – LEAVE – PRECINCTS – TEMPLE – NOTHING – SEEDED – EYE – HYGEIA – HAVEN ROOM – REALITY – TIME – DOCTOR – AGAIN – INCUBATING – PEERING – EYES – VISION – ENTER – TRIUMPH – THINK – BABY – ASLEEP.

Other poems exploring mother to child relationships include *Genetics, Effects, On her Blindness* and *You, Shiva, and my Mum,* the last of which also includes a meeting with a god. The meditative, philosophical nature of **Out of the Bag** could be compared with *History* and its concern with the significance of the past. Its use of regular form containing and framing irregularity could connect it to *The War Correspondent.*

# Alan Jenkins, *effects*

According to one of Alan Jenkins' poetic 'elders and betters' his 'subject was loss' and he should 'stay with that'. He certainly stays with it in *Effects*, a poem of devastating everyday observation and desolate loss. Now, while the 'I' voice in the poem could most obviously be identified with Jenkins himself it need not be seen as so personal. Either way, the personal voice intensifies the universality of the experience. The effects of the title are not released, mimetically, until the very last line of this 50-line meditation, but the poetic effects are felt from the unsettling first line with its 'scarred' 'hand'. Emily Dickinson insisted that 'art is a house that tries to be haunted' and here Jenkins achieves the type of lingering literature that Dickinson would admire.

## 1

### Ephemeral effects

This haunting quality produced by the poem derives from its everyday trivialities, which become torqued into something greater through Jenkins' transformative verse. Not only is the subject matter difficult to confront but the manner of Jenkins' poetic exploration is also deeply unsettling. I suppose this is very much the point. Nowhere is this more acute than in his unavoidable message about the distinctly ephemeral nature of our existence.

The poem condenses the aging process his mother endures through the detailed descriptions of her hands. The poem begins with her 'scarred' hand,

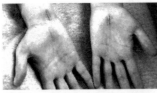 testifying to her durability, her enduring strength, the triumph of the physical over reality. Rather than weakness, such scars celebrate the robustness of a body capable of withstanding years of 'shopping,' 'slicing' and 'scrubbing'. Whilst undeniably domestic, the poem suggests a quiet heroism in the everyday as these trivial tribulations originate from 'love', albeit an 'old-fashioned' love, but love nevertheless.

The alliteration of 'I held her hand' with its softness resurfaces much later in the poem in line 44 in a subtle, yet vitally, different way. It becomes 'the hand I held,' which immediately implies a compelling change through the loss of the previous possessive pronoun 'her.' Such a minute difference dehumanises the mother figure, the hand becoming a mere object. By this stage in the poem, the strong 'scarred' hands of the beginning have 'become blotched and crinkled,' two adjectives that foreground their poor condition and delicacy. The connotations of 'crinkled', in particular, imply a paper-like quality that captures her intense vulnerability just before death.

## 2

### Sentimental synecdoche

A fancy Greek term for how the part can be substituted for the whole (i.e. 'sails' for 'ships' and 'suits' for 'business types') the poem excels in its equation of mundane everyday objects with the recently deceased. Jenkins vividly captures how ordinary personal effects can contain such latent power through their ability to store vast reservoirs of memory.

The speaker will not have access to the hands of his beloved mother in the future. But he/she will have the things that adorned them: 'her rings' and her 'classic ladies' model, gold strap' 'watch'. Both items replace the mother after death's annihilating effect. In fact, the mini-mystery of the watch that 'was gone' propels the poem into a series of episodic accounts that convey her descent into senility. Jenkins uses anaphora (the repetition of 'not' at the start of poetic lines) as a stimulus to memorialisation. Seeing the dead mother's hand without the 'gold strap' watch compels the speaker to think of that same hand with the watch.

The sequence of memories triggered by the watchless hand is a heart-breaking condensation of the mother's abject loneliness: From the death of her husband, to her 'scotch' soaked failure to cope, to her admittance to 'the psychiatric ward'. The poem ends by bestowing huge value on 'the little bag of her effects'. Their value does not come from their status as independent objects in their own right; rather it is their dependence on their previous owner that renders them valuable. Essentially worthless personal effects become repositories of the past, makers of memory that bring the dead back to life, if only in the most figurative of ways.


## 3

### The taste of disdain

The oddly sour relationship between the mother and child is conspicuous in *Effects*. The poet is unflinching in his refusal to idealise the deceased; there are no funereal clichés such as 'she was the best mum a son could ever have'. Admirably, the minutiae of life are depicted as sharply and realistically as those of aging and death. The reality of their relationship is characterised by the son's 'disdain' and 'contempt' for his mother.

The speaker's mother is 'old-fashioned' and backwards in her insistence on 'bland' 'English' cuisine. She has not, and presumably cannot, move with the times. This is a woman who embodies the narrow spirit of the Little Englander, in how she prefers the 'familiar flavours' of the 'bland' to 'funny foreign stuff'. Jenkins' wealth of f-sounds introduces an element of the conflict between the two. Her designation of anywhere outside England as 'abroad', which Jenkins is careful to put into speech marks, suggests a closed-minded woman stuck in the past. Her voice is captured in tiny, trivial soundbites that capture her ordinariness.

Not that the speaker comes across as noble character either. The poem is surprisingly candid in this regard. Here we have a man full of snobbish 'disdain' and 'contempt' for a woman no more to blame for being a product of her time than he is. Telling little details like when he confesses to 'all the weeks I didn't come' in the traumatic loss of her husband betray a cold, uncaring personality. Even when he recognises her domestic toil as 'giving love the only way she knew' he cannot help his 'disdain' for her backward ways and unsophisticated interests. Most damning is the heartrending moment at the end of the poem where she begs him to *'Please don't leave'*. Jenkins' only italicisation of her speech and also his use of a forceful molossus [three stressed beats in a row] maximises the vulnerability of her distress. Tellingly, this is deflated by the casual admission: 'But of course I left'. There is something too barbed about the mother's remark about how he 'grew up and learned contempt' that implies intense disappointment with the adult speaker. Not only do we get access to his disdain, but also her disdain at his disdain. It is clear that both characters in this intense drama cannot see each other without personal resentment: Jenkins places emphasis on the inability to not see through subtle repetition and variation of language i.e. 'stared unseeing', 'gulped and unseeing', 'blinked unseeing' and 'blinked and stared'. Symbolically at the end of the poem the mother 'could not [...] turn her face to see' her returning son, which implies that reconciliation never happened.

However, despite their acrimonious relationship and the lack of reconciliation, there is clearly an intense sense of bereavement. Death seems to defuse the personal antagonisms that life simply could not. Some sort of regret at this situation is suggested in how the speaker reconstructs the pathos of her demise. It is almost as if empathy is only possible after she has passed on. The painful details of her existence on the 'psychiatric ward' are nightmarish in their portrayal of an undignified, dehumanising purgatory: TVs 'blare' to mask deranged 'moans and curses'; the patients 'shuffled round, and drooled, and swore...'. Caesuras, created by the commas, imply an awkward pausing as if the speaker finds it difficult to recount such horrors. More worryingly, the ellipsis at the end of this line allows this recounting to trail off into a guilty silence as if hiding even more horrifying details.

**4**

**The echoes of memory**

Jenkins' poem uses form to reinforce the reality of memorialising the dead. There is no place here for stately, elegiac formal patterns that bring the consolation of predictable consistency. Instead, his form espouses a regular unpredictability. While the 50 lines are written invariably in an iambic metre, this shifts from tetrameter to hexameter. The most striking formal aspect is the complex, sinuous rhyme scheme Jenkins employs. It is hard to describe completely, but the poem can be broken down into three long sections where some sort of rhyme scheme is discernible and a short final section where mono-rhyme is used conspicuously.

The rhyme scheme in these longer sections is curiously unpredictable. It is simultaneously tight and loose: Just when the ear is starting to accommodate itself to a definite pattern the poem shifts suddenly into new sounds before lurching back to previous ones. For example, take the first 9 lines. The end rhymes are: **SCARRED – WAIT – RAW – PLATE – KNEW – STEW – ATE – RINGS**, which gives a rhyme scheme of **ABCABDDBE**. There are outbursts of cross rhyme i.e. **SWORE – BAND – WORE – HAND – MORE**. Again, the ear expects a word that rhymes with 'hand' and 'band' but gets 'sleeve' instead. Additionally, Jenkins uses half-rhymes like **SCARRED** and **ABROAD** and **IF** and **WIFE** to further emphasis a woozy soundscape that seems to drift in and out of sonic focus. All in all, it gives the poem an echoing sonic unpredictability that seems to mimic the senile memory or maybe just the uncertainty of memory itself. Like a sonic déjà vu, the sound patterns feel familiar but different. Yet there are sudden bursts of clarity.

The use of sporadic mono-rhyming couplets and finally a triplet allow brief respites of certainty from the shifting sonic uncertainty that characterises the poem as a whole. In this way they mimic the memories stimulated by 'the little bag of effects' and by all objects with sentimental value. They also mimic the sudden moments of clarity experienced by the senile. Such instances are important as they can be seen to condense down the entire poem to its basic elements: **KNEW** and **STEW**; **GONE** and **ON**; **SAT** and **AT**; **SCOTCH** and **TOUCH**; **SLEEVE** and **LEAVE**; **SHE**, **SEE** and **ME**. Perhaps, fittingly, the most certainty comes at the end of the poem, where the aforementioned cross-rhyming sequence segues into a mono-rhyming couplet and triplet. Jenkins' end rhymes here suggest that the only certainty we have is death and loss.

**Crunches**

SCARRED – KNIVES – RAW – REDDENED – SAUCEPAN – LOVE – MEAT
– OLD-FASHIONED – RINGS – DRAWER – FADED – SCENT-SPRAYS –
'ABROAD' – NEVER – WIFE – WATCH – GONE – NEVER – YEARS –
SOAPS – COOK – ENGLISH – FAMILIAR – FOREIGN – YOUNG – SAT –
UNSEEING – INNER – HEAVED – SCOTCH – TOUCH – AGAIN – WARD –
BLINKED – DREAMT – GIRL – CONTEMPT – BLARED – MOANS – PILLS
– DROOLED – LAY – SMUDGED – CRINKLED – CLASP – FUMBLE –
PLEASE – BACK – FACE – EFFECTS

**A further crunch:**

SCARRED – LOVE – OLD-FASHIONED – RINGS – FADED – WIFE –
GONE – YEARS – FAMILIAR – SCOTCH – WARD – DREAMT – BLARED –
MOANS – PILLS – DROOLED – FUMBLE – PLEASE – FACE – EFFECTS

An obvious connecting poem for **Effects** is Adam Thorpe's **On Her Blindness**, which also explores the specific loss of an aging mother. Other poems featuring relationships with mothers include, **Material**, **Genetics** and **Out of the Bag** while **Inheritance** shifts the perspective to a parent's point of view. A different type of loss haunts Sean O'Brien's elegiac **Fantasia on a Theme of James Wright**.

## Robert Minhinnick, *the fox in the national library of Wales*

**1**

### Foxiness

According to the **Cambridge Dictionary of Literary Symbols, second edition**, our association of foxes with cunning and trickery can be traced back to the Ancient Greeks. The playwright Aristophanes, for instance, used 'foxiness' several times to mean trickery. Foxes also feature in Aesop's Fables as well as in medieval stories featuring Reynard the Fox. Much later in literary history, the Elizabethan writer, Ben Johnson's play about cunning deception, *Volpone,* is subtitled **The Fox**. A modern poet would not be able to write a poem about a fox without being aware of the animal's significance in the work of one of the monumental poets of the twentieth century, Ted Hughes. In particular, Hughes' **The Thought-Fox** is very widely known. In Hughes' poetry the fox is a totemic animal associated with the mysterious forces of the imagination and inspiration and specifically with poetry itself. The prints of the fox on the snow in *The Though-Fox*, for instance, become the words printed on the page of the poem. And, of course, there is also Roald

Dahl's *Fantastic Mr Fox*. Minhinnick would be very aware that his central symbol comes with a long trail of literary associations, both ancient and modern.

## 2

### An eclectic museum

Minhinnick's poem depicts the fleeting experiences with different time frames, historical contexts and social customs that happen when you pass through a museum quickly. There are aspects of the narrative that are almost novelistic - for example, the gathering together seemingly disparate stories and the binding them into one wide-reaching narrative (poetry, of course, can do this too). Minhinnick's poetry often explores ideas of cultural identity, particularly Welshness. It is interesting that, although this is the National Museum of Wales, its contents span vast periods and locations. For instance, the museum includes artefacts from China, India and France. Perhaps this rich variety invites us to consider how far culture is a composite – Welsh nationality constructed through its interaction with other cultures. It also raises questions about whether the preservation is always accurate and fair to those who are part of its history. Alternatively, such diversity could suggest that the purpose of a national museum is to gather evidence of the 'other', examples of far-flung objects that help define 'Welshness' through comparison.

Different museums arrange their collections in varying ways. The conscious arrangement of history indicates the curator's specific attitude towards preservation, presentation and organisation of the past. For example, whilst the Victoria and Albert Museum in London organises by time period (for example, Ancient Greece), the Pitt Rivers Museum in Oxford organises its some half a million objects by geographical or cultural areas.

Whatever organisational principle governs exhibits at the National Museum of Wales, the fox ignores and disrupts it. One moment he is in 'Photography' the next he's in the 'Folk Studies Department'; briefly sniffing at a 'dodo', the next moment he's 'at the door of Celtic orthography'. If the fox is a kind of guide to the museum he takes us on a rather idiosyncratic, difficult-to -follow route.

**3**

**The fox magician**

The fox (which, itself, could be read as a metaphor for the poetic narrative passing through events in time) touches lightly upon a vast range of events from human history. In doing so, it introduces new and varied times and spaces, which together form a mutable and flexible feeling of historic progression. Magically the symbolic fox is simultaneously 'in the fossils and the folios', rendering the time periods themselves mere pieces of information, since the fossil has now been lifted out of geological history and placed concurrently with the man-made folios. By its very presence, the fox lifts

objects and artefacts out of history, joining them and making them part of the poem's narrative. The objects described in the poem - 'the dodo', 'the grave-goods, the chariots, the gods of darkness', exist in their own narrative and also in the fox's.

There are multiple possibilities for what the fox could represent; apart from the comparisons we have already drawn between the fox and the poetic narrative itself, the fox is, as we have also said, often a symbol for cunning and motivation. The fact that he is in a museum, then, is a curious one - is there something that the fox is trying to find, as if he's on a hunt? On closer examination, it would seem that the journey the fox takes is actually far more interesting than the destination; the fox goes all the way from 'the feet of Jesus' through 'the tear in Dante's cloak', passing 'an age in a footfall'. His destination is unknown - and his identity itself is kept secret, as 'No one else /has seen him yet. /But they are closing /the iron doors'. The slightly disjointed penultimate stanza, with its excited flurry of 'f' alliteration, indicates an otherworldliness, a mystic or fantastical nature to the fox:

**'I will tell you this. /He is something to follow, /this red fellow. /This fox I foster- /he is the future.'**

Notice the close weave of sounds in these short, swift-stepping lines. In addition to the thread of alliteration, 'tell' is echoed in fell(ow), 'follow' half-rhymes with 'fellow' and 'foster' half-rhymes 'future'. The fact that the fox does not go 'in for the kill', as we might expect with a fox on the prowl, is surprising; clearly he has more important things to find.

The narrator talks about the fox as if it is a magician: The narrator has 'legged' it after the fox's 'legerdemain'; the fox transgresses the bounds of time, 'passes an age in a footfall' and space (being in two places at once) and he's invisible to everyone except the narrator (is he, perhaps, a figment or externalisation of the narrator's imagination?). The alliterative repetitiveness of the language creates the same kind of misdirection a magician might use to distract the audience from the substance of what is really going on - 'for at a foxtrot travels this fox /backwards and forwards in the museum'. The narrative itself, through its kaleidoscopic and sometimes seeming crude sonic stitching together of so many different eras and objects, makes the weight of the museum's history flimsy, strange and surreal. This is the effect of the fox.

In Celtic legend, the fox is believed to be a guide and is honoured for its wisdom. Maybe this is why 'He is something to follow, /this red fellow'. Apparently, the elusive fox has access to a higher knowledge not necessarily known to us. It's certainly not known to the narrator.

If this mercurial fox is a guide, what do you think he is leading us to?

**4**

**Our curious narrator**

It is something of a surprise when the 'I' voice appears suddenly in the third stanza. Who is this person who came 'as quickly' as he could? Is he the museum's curator, or a caretaker, perhaps? In the fourth stanza he sounds the alarm in a peculiarly ineffectual way:

**'The fox is in the fossils and the folios, I cry'**

Try shouting that line or the next one quickly. They're far too wordy and too alliterative to sound properly like speech. The fantastical flurry of 'f's continues throughout a stanza in which each line starts with the same four monosyllables. Together this generates a surging sense of momentum and urgency, enhanced by the emphatic rhythm and the repetition of the last lines:

**'The fox is in the flock**
**The fox is in the flock'**

But then what happens? Nothing. The surge and swell of urgency immediately dissipates. Through the next five stanzas the fox moves unhurriedly and unimpeded on his journey. What is our curator/ caretaker/ narrator figure doing in the meantime?

When he next appears this character's language is a curious mix of the colloquial and the erudite. 'I legged it', 'after his legerdemain'. How long he has been chasing this fox could imply time within the poem's narrative – while the fox has shimmying and foxtrotting at will this character has been hopelessly trying to catch him, but it might also suggest following the fox over a much longer time period, as if the narrator has been tracking the path of the quicksilver fox all his life. Though the narrator does not resolve the mysterious significance of the fox he does tells us it is 'something to follow', like a political belief or religious conviction. And he uses a curious verb 'this fox I **foster**'. 'Foster' as in bring up, nurture, develop. This attitude doesn't seem to fit with his earlier hue and cry. Unless, that is, the fox has performed a kind of enchantment, cast a spell on our curious narrator. Starting off chasing the fox, he ends up following it.

**5**

**The fox-poet**

Ted Hughes' *The Thought-Fox* appeared in his first collection, **The Hawk in the Rain**. As we have noted, Hughes' fox is widely analysed as a symbol for the act of writing a poem, words set onto page like its 'neat prints into the snow'. Just as the fox in the museum is the thin thread uniting disparate eras and cultures, and which guides us through the narrative, Hughes' fox is the thread weaving through the poetic imagination to lead us to the writing of the poem itself. This fox leaves his mark when 'the page is printed', the passing of time marked as 'the clock ticks'. Furthermore, just as Hughes' fox's paw-prints create the words left behind on the paper, Minhinnick's fox leaves 'Between dynasties... footprints [which] have still to fade, between the Shan and the Yang'. Both foxes leave poetry behind them.

Interestingly, the passage of the elusive, transgressive fox is tethered to the stanzas. Though the stanzas and the lengths of lines within them are highly irregular, and despite the pervasive use of enjambment within them, each stanza is closed off and sealed with an emphatic full stop. Not a single line steps over from one stanza to another. The pattern of the stanzas is also interesting. Take the first stanza, for instance. This starts regularly in jaunty iambic tetrameter:

**'He scans the frames but doesn't stop'**

But immediately after the first metrical foot of the next line the even pattern is disrupted - 'who has come to the' - and the metrical pulse is lost. This quatrain recovers a sense of sonic order in its final two lines. Coupled with the use of clearly unstressed function words, alliteration in the last line makes the beats on 'brush' and 'Baroque' emphatic and the anapaestic pattern helps the line to skip along briskly. The envelope rhyme scheme ('stop' and 'Baroque'), though slightly disrupted by the internal rhyme of 'fox', adds to the re-imposition of sonic order.

This restoration is, however, short-lived. Ditching metre and rhyme, the six line second stanza follows an entirely different, irregular pattern. And so the poem goes on, each stanza following a different pattern to its predecessor. In short, the introduction of the fox in the second line of the poem brings with it transgressive forces of disorder, forces that yoke together disparate things - pair the 'dodo', for example, randomly with 'Celtic orthography', 'fossils' randomly with 'folios' - and subvert the orderly arrangement of museum

69

collections, and of stanzas. Running against this creative disorderliness are counter forces, such as those hard-pressed full stops. The musicality of Minhinnick's language, and the self-assuredness with which the poem's momentum is gathered and then released in waves, mirrors both the physical movements and athleticism of the fox. But it also imposes control over the very same slippery and shiny creature. The fantastical fox, a metaphor for poetic imagination, forms the narrative progression, but 'he' is also at the service of it; both the fox and the poem grow and develop simultaneously, mutually dependent.

**The Fox in the National Museum of Wales** crunched:

**FOX – MUSEUM – RENAISSANCE – BAROQUE – DYNASTIES – FOOTPRINTS – PORCELAIN – REVOLUTION – MOLECULE – FOSSILS – FOLIOS – FOX – FLUX – FLOCK – DODO – CELTIC – GODS – SKELETON – ORDOVICIAN – CUBISTS – SURREALISTS – SILVER – ICELAND – JESUS – DANTE – LABYRINTH – FOLLOW – FELLOW – FUTURE – CLOSING – DOORS**

Another poem using the conceit of a constantly shifting and moving animal with **The Fox...** is **Dürer's Hare**. Within the Forward selection, for the theme of preserving and exploring history, we could compare **Inheritance, The War Correspondent, History** and **Effects**. Transgressive, magical creatures also appear in **Giuseppe, The Gun** and **The Lammas Hireling**.

# Sinéad Morrissey, *genetics*

Describe the poetic form of a villanelle in words and it sounds fiendishly difficult to write. Here are the authors of **The Making of a Poem, a Norton Anthology of Poetic Forms** giving it their best shot:

'Five stanzas occur of three lines each. They are followed by a stanza, a quatrain, of four lines. This is common to all villanelles. The first line of the first stanza serves as the last line of the second and fourth stanzas. The third line of the first stanza serves as the last line of the third and fifth stanzas. And these two refrain lines reappear to constitute the last two lines of the closing quatrain...The rhyme scheme is aba, for the first three lines of the poem. And these rhymes reappear to match and catch the refrains, throughout the villanelle. The first line of the first stanza rhymes with the third line of the fourth stanza. And so on.' [7]

 Got it? Good. So your task now is to write your own villanelle. Except that even the complex form of the villanelle seems to have bewitched even the august authors of the Norton guide. Because that's not quite right. The rhyme scheme in a villanelle is, indeed, aba, but this scheme runs through all the five three line, tercet, stanzas before finally being recycled in the concluding two lines. In other words, all the rhymes in a villanelle are composed from just two rhyme sounds. Lines, 1, 3, 4, 6, 7, 9, 10, 12, 13, 15, 16, 18 & 19 all rhyme with each other. The middle lines of each tercet, lines 2, 5, 8, 11, 14 and 17, also all rhyme with each other. Clearer now? Good. So your task in to write your own villanelle. Except that, we think it's much easier to appreciate the form of a villanelle through a visual representation, thus:

---

[7] Strand & Boland, *The Making of a Poem*, p. 7

| Line 1 | A | 1st refrain |
| Line 2 | B | |
| Line 3 | A | 2nd refrain |
| | | |
| Line 4 | A | |
| Line 5 | B | |
| Line 6 | A | 1st refrain (same as line 1) |
| | | |
| Line 7 | A | |
| Line 8 | B | |
| Line 9 | A | 2nd refrain (same as line 3) |
| | | |
| Line 10 | A | |
| Line 11 | B | |
| Line 12 | A | 1st refrain (same as lines 1 & 6) |
| | | |
| Line 13 | A | |
| Line 14 | B | |
| Line 15 | A | 2nd refrain (same as lines 3 & 9) |
| | | |
| Line 16 | A | |
| Line 17 | B | |
| Line 18 | A | 1st refrain (same as lines 1,6 & 12) |
| Line 19 | A | 2nd refrain (same as lines 3, 9 & 15) |

Righto. Now you've seen the form, time for you...except that, it helps to try to think of a suitable subject that might fit this elegant, looping dance of a form with its repeated patterns of lines. What we need is a subject in which there is a lot of repetition, but with variations. How about a school day? And though the form looks devilishly difficult, actually once you've got your first three lines you've already written nearly half your poem, including the last two lines. I find it helpful to write these lines in once you've got your first three in place.

And this is how I'd teach Morrissey's poem. Give the students the title and the first stanza only:

**'My father's in my fingers, but my mother's in my palms.**
**I lift them up and look at them with pleasure –**
**I know my parents made me by my hands.'**

So, now we can also slot lines 6, 9,1 2, 15, 18 & 19 into their fixed place in the scheme. We have our two rhyme sounds, 'a' and 'er'. Noticeably Morrissey has already bent the sound a little, or subverted the form a touch, with the assonantal rhyme 'hands' not quite harmonising with the first long 'a' sound. Why might she have done this? Certainly the slight dissonance suits the topic; the poet is trying to bring together parents who have grown apart. There's a suggestion of slight tension in the poem's sound world. Brought together in their daughter, the parents are also modified in her. So, the poem's rhymes encode the sense of continuity, but also change.

Before going on to fill in the blank lines of the poem, it's worth stopping and discussing the first tercet in more detail. Though the language looks straightforward enough, a gently surreal quality is generated by semantic ambiguity. For example, initially the apostrophes seem to indicate possession and so two nouns appear to be missing. My father's something - 'pen' perhaps? The mildly disorientating effect is sustained in the second line with ambiguous referencing of the twice used pronoun 'them'. Do the two 'thems' refer to the same thing/ person? A number of different possible meaning are kept in play. <u>Which of the following do you think is most convincing?</u>

- I lift the things belonging to my father and mother and look at these
- I lift my hands and look at my hands
- I lift my parents and look at my parents
- I lift my hands and look at my parents

It's only in the last line that the ambiguity is

resolved. We realise that the apostrophes are not working to indicate possession but instead to abbreviate the nouns, so that the sense is 'my father is in my fingers'. But there's still a curious, surreal feel here; how can your father be 'in' your fingers or your mother 'in' your palms?

Now you might well be thinking I'm making quite a meal of this. And you could well be right. But I do think it's striking that although Morrissey uses very straightforward diction she manages to make language elusive, hard to pin down in terms of meanings. The double use of 'them' implies that there is no difference between her hands and her parents, they are both simply 'them'. And the overt sentiment of the poem is that her parents can be reunited in her hands. This semantic slipperiness, like the half-rhyme, conveys a counter current or undercurrent in the poem that suggests reconciliation may not be so easy, or perhaps signals the poet's awareness that the reconciliation she achieves is not completely convincing.

It's worth noting too how Morrissey flexes the villanelle form a little. With only two rhyme sounds to play with, rhymes can rather stick out awkwardly from a villanelle, making the language sound unnatural, clunky and too contrived. In an unsubtly written villanelle we will hit and notice the rhymes too much. Morrissey uses enjambment to bed down and tuck in her rhymes, so that the sentence runs over the end of the line and into the next one. In fact the first enjambment runs stanza four into stanza five. Half-rhymes also help to dampen down the sonic echoing in the poem. The trick is to bend the form so that, despite its rigidity, it can carry the cadences of a spoken voice. Morrissey pulls off this trick with great technical aplomb.

So, now it's the students turn to flesh out the skeleton of Morrissey's poem and then to write their own villanelle on the suggested subject of a school day. By way of encouragement the author has had a go himself and you can find my villanelle at the back of this book. No peeking though, not until you've had a go yourself.

Morrissey's poem sets itself out in a series of declarative statements, seemingly coolly explicating how the narrator has inherited her parents' genes and how these are evident in her body. Hence in some ways, the poem's logic tells us, the parents continue to be married in their daughter. The dominant punctuation mark is the full stop which outnumbers commas. End-stopped lines, emphasised with full stops, give each statement a definite, factual air:

**'My body is their marriage register.**
**I re-enact their wedding with my hands'**

This re-enactment even turns back time. When the narrator turns her hands into a church, her mother and father appear as if by magic, 'demure before a priest reciting psalms'. As the poem progresses the repeated refrains of the form work together like rhetorical devices - piling up they insist that reconciliation has taken place.

<u>Why did Morrissey choose the conceit of the hands as a church?</u> I think she made this choice because the 'here is a church, here is a steeple' rhyme is associated with small children. Isn't there something small childish in the poem's wish-fulfilment of reuniting parents who have grown apart? In the poem itself her parents are, indeed, reconciled. But they probably were not in real life. Hence the elegant poem is made poignant through contrast with reality. <u>Why did the poet choose the form of the villanelle to tackle this subject?</u> The form of a villanelle is like a formal dance - lines are rotated,

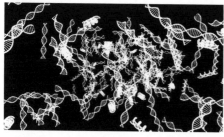 separate and then join back up again. Lines one and three for instance start close, circle each other and finish even closer together as the poem's last two lines. Hence the form embodies the idea of separating and coming back together again; separation and connection between the narrator's parents and between them and her. Perhaps there's even some analogy between the poem's shape and the twists of a genetic code. The narrator is also stuck in the desire to reconcile her parents, a

repeating emotional pattern; a need she cannot escape or move beyond. At least not until the final stanza where there's a major shift in the poem.

There is a delayed introduction of an addressee 'you' into *Genetics*. Reading the last stanza, we realise the whole poem has, in fact, been addressed to this silent presence and that the villanelle form is being employed rhetorically, to persuade this person about something important. This much is apparent from the fact that the final stanza begins with a conjunction 'so', a simple synonym for 'therefore'. This is the language of logical argument: A proposition has been advanced, demonstrated and proven and so this final stanza proffers the logical conclusion. The persuasiveness continues with the shift into imperatives. And we realise that *Genetics* is in fact a tender love poem, to the poet's parents, but also to their lover. An offer is made to be with someone and perhaps have a child with them. The tone and manner of the poem might appear cool and sophisticated; a clever conceit is manufactured from a childish rhyme and is elegantly achieved. But underneath this cleverness there's a vulnerability, a sense of loss, a poignant tenderness. And that too is persuasive.

***Genetics* crunched:**

**MY – THEM – PARENTS – REPELLED – SEPARATE – TOUCH –NOTHING – IMAGE – LEAST – SHAPE – I – MY – PARENT – MANAGE – SO – FUTURE – BEQUEATH - MAKE**

Obviously in terms of theme **_Genetics_** could be compared with **Inheritance** and **Material.** Other poems about relationships with parents include **On her Blindness** and **Effects.** In terms of innovative use of a closed poetic form, **Ode to a Grayson Perry Urn** would make an interesting comparison.

# Andrew Motion, *from the journal of a disappointed man*

## 1

This is a poem about being suspended, about being stuck in an uncertain, in-between, or liminal, state. Take the title. This informs us that the text is an extract taken from a longer piece of non-fiction. That seems straightforward enough. However a 'journal' usually comprises factual reportage written in prose, but, this text is a poem. Moreover, check Motion's oeuvre and you'll discover that there is no extended poetic 'journal' from which this piece has been extracted. The journal of the title is, in fact, fictional. Such tricksy unreliability should put us on guard as readers – from the outset we cannot necessarily trust what we are being told in this poem, however transparent the language might appear. Uncertainty about the nature of the text raises questions too about its narrator: If we cannot rely even on the title how can we trust the testimony that follows? Is the titular character Motion himself, or a fictional alter ego? Many questions are raised in this poem, but answers are withheld. Hence the reader, like the wooden pile being lifted, and the narrator himself, is left up in the air.

The poem's 'action' confirms the theme of suspension and stasis. Though much thought and rumination goes on in the poem - about how to move the pile into the right place - it actually remains in the same place as it started in the opening lines. The 'action' of the poem is actually 'inaction'.

**2**

**'As clear as water'**

Prosaic language invites us to lower our reading guard. This appears to be language as a window – to be looked through, not at. Immediately a chatty colloquial style is established: 'I discovered these men...'. The speaker clumsily repeats words and phrases; the second sentence includes, 'and, as I said' and a 'wooden pile, a massive affair'. Such close unnecessary repetition is a feature often found in spoken language. It would have been simple for the poet to straighten out the syntax to avoid awkward repetition. For example:

**'I discovered these men driving a massive new wooden pile into the pier'**

The syntactical clumsiness is, then, deliberate. The apparent artlessness of the style is designed to win our trust, invite our belief, perhaps. Other aspects of the language enhance this impression. This is plain, limpid language, stripped of any ornamentation. There is, for instance, a distinct absence of figurative imagery. And, though the poem is arranged in neat looking quatrains, it reads like prose. We have no problems decoding the sense. There's no rhyme scheme either nor any rhythmical pulse. Few sonic effects distract (or hold) our attention. No poetic enchantment is going on here, it seems. Motion appears to be doing no more than using ordinary, unremarkable language to inform us about an ordinary, unremarkable incident. There's something flat and mechanical about it all. Look, for instance, at his use of bland, colourless adjectives: 'powerful', 'silent', 'close', 'great', 'whole', 'slow'.

Seemingly clumsy repetitions continue:
- 'massive' is used twice in quick succession when it would have been easy to select a synonym. It is also recycled later in the poem
- words such as 'pile', 'swinging', 'say', 'water', 'tired' are also repeated
- 'men' is employed three times in very close proximity: 'even the men'; 'very powerful men'; '...silent men'
- the empty intensifier 'very', the sort of word one is told never to use in

poetry, is employed in a way that deliberately draws our attention: 'very powerful men/ very ruminative'.

Motion has written about aiming to make the language of his poem's 'as clear as water'. Certainly the language in this poem appears straightforward, literal, transparent.

And this seems a dangerous strategy – the wattage of the poem is turned down so low that we might be tempted not to bother reading on or to read deeper. If we were judge a poem by its number of striking or memorable lines, we wouldn't judge this one very highly.

The narrator's language is, however, clearly educated: He uses words such as 'nevertheless', 'ruminative', 'trajectory' and 'eclipse'. His social class is also signalled through his reference to a gob of spit as a 'bolus' and to one of the men as a 'fellow'. There is a marked contrast between the inactive observer and silent working men he watches and comments upon. They are men of action; he is a thoughtful, reflective sort of chap. The masculine physicality of the men is emphasised; they are 'massive', 'strong', 'heavy'. However, though observer and  observed seem to have little in common they are both left in the air at the end of the poem, unable to complete whatever they are each doing.

**3**

**Look, no tricks**

Nothing much actually happens in the poem and there is nothing much of great interest that is happening within the prosaic language of the poem. And nothing much is being said in the scene depicted either. It's a virtual dumb show. This is emphasised through repetition: 'silent men'; 'speech was not something to interest them'; 'still saying nothing', 'no one spoke'. So at the heart of the poem is silence as well as inaction, another sort of stasis and suspense. There's something postmodern going on here, as if the poem's inside out. It's also an inside out kind of journal - conventionally journals record significant events, when something happens. This journal records an incident where nothing much seems to happen.

In Samuel Beckett's play **Waiting for Godot** (depicted above) the playwright made inaction the central action. Famously nothing happens in *Waiting for Godot*, twice – once in the first half and once in the second. Two tramps wait for the eponymous Godot to arrive, which, of course, he never does. Similarly the composer John Cage's *'4'3"'* comprises four and a half minutes of silence. At a performance of this piece musicians sit on stage, tune up and then play nothing at all. It is the silence the audience listen to. Or rather they listen to the noises that fill the silence and this comprises the piece's music.

In Motion's poem characters gather, as if for a play, equipment hangs ready in place, the poem's narrator forms an audience; silence and stillness fall. And then nothing happens. However, whereas Cage's piece sensitises an audience to every sound, making them conscious of the act of listening itself, no analogous pay-off on the act of reading is achieved in Motion's poem. We are, perhaps, made conscious of the role of narrating through the repetition of phrases that foreground this role; 'no one said what they saw'; 'I cannot say what'; 'I should say'; 'silent on the subject'. And that seems to be it.

**4**

What then is the point of this poem, if indeed a poem needs a point? Well, it appears to me to be a kind of loose extended metaphor for the experience of writer's block. It's not as specific as an allegory, but there's a correspondence between the elements of this narrative and the process of writing a poem:

- the powerful men, the agents who could make this happen, are analogous to the forces of the intellect
- the equipment of chains, hawser and so forth analogous to the resources of language
- the puzzling over a great difficulty equals the struggle to write
- the silence suggests a concentrated state of mind, but also blankness
- the new pile, hanging mid-air is an analogue for the poem itself.

Read this way, the neat trick of the poem is turn the inability to write, the writer's block and its attendant silence, stasis and suspension, into its own subject. Ironically then, not being able to write becomes the subject of writing.

This explanation also helps, arguably, to account for the otherwise incongruous references to the men as 'monsters', to the foreman's 'majesty' and to the hyperbolic sounding 'crack of doom'. If we accept the writing block analogy, then these words express the poet's intense, difficult feelings about writing. Similarly, in this light, the line 'tired, so tired of the whole business' expresses the poet's frustration with what in *East Coker* T. S. Eliot called 'the intolerable wrestle/ with words and meanings'. Andrew Motion has said that his 'poems are the product of a relationship between a side of my mind which is conscious, alert, educated and manipulative, and a side which is as murky as a primaeval swamp. I can't predict when this relationship will flower. If I try to goad it into existence I merely engage with one side of my mind or the other, and the poem suffers.' Applying this, we suggest *From the Journal...* dramatises the failed attempt of the conscious, educated side of the poet's mind to access, connect and engage with the mysterious murkiness of his subconscious inner swamp.

*From the Journal... crunched*

DISCOVERED – PARAPHENALIA – CRANES – PILE – OVER – MASSIVE – POWERFUL – SILENT – SPEECH – IF – MONOSYLLABLES – NEVERTHELESS – OBSCURE – EDGE – STRENGTH – DIFFICULTY – CANNOT – SILENT – REALISED – TIRED – NOTHING – STRONG – CARED – DOOM – SHOULD – JUSTICE – SECRET – CEASED – ABANDONED – POSITION – MYSTIC – NO-ONE – FELLOW – BOLUS – TOBACCO – DESCENT – FOREMAN – TENSION – MAJESTY – AWAY – ECLIPSE – CLOSED – FOLLOWED – MID-AIR

A literary academic, influential poetry editor, ex poet laureate and biographer of Philip Larkin, Andrew Motion is strongly associated with The Movement and its aesthetics. *From the Journal of a Disappointed Man* has many characteristics that connect the poem with The Movement style: There's the neat, conventional arrangement of stanzas into regular quatrains; the use of ordinary, pared down 'real' language to describe a real experience; there's the characteristic poet in the role of wry ironic observer of modern life. Motion has, however, updated the aesthetic by being more self-conscious about the act of narrating. He's created a character of the 'disappointed man' who is like a version of a Movement poet, but at one, ironic, self-reflexive remove from the poet himself. In terms of the other poems in the Forward anthology, stylistically there's common ground with Barber's *Material* and Dunmore's *To My Nine-Year-Old Self.* The liminal inbetweeness links the poem to *Copus' An Easy Passage* while the self-conscious observatory role is reminiscent of Boyle's *A Leisure Centre is also a Temple of Learning.*

An interesting and sophisticated comparison could be made with *Out of the Bag.* In Heaney's poem inspiration springs from encounters with external, mythical or sublime forces - the equivalent of Motion's encounter with something 'primeval'. In Motion's poem, though all the apparatus is assembled encounter is missing, yet the poem is still completed. Mostly this comparison would work through productive contrast.

# Daljit Nagra: *look we have coming to Dover!*

## 1

Beware the intolerant Daily Mail reader! Beware the grammatical pedant! This poem is going to make you feel quite queasy indeed... Daljit Nagra is an English poet from a Punjabi heritage who uses the unfamiliar Punjabi patois to animate the soundscapes of his poems. Thematically, he is sensitive to both the plurality and duality of his Englishness, where he highlights the struggle to reconcile concepts of England and India as well as inside and outside. *Look we have coming to Dover!* however rewinds time to when his parents and countless others sailed to England in hope of a life 'so various, so beautiful, so new...' to quote Nagra's quotation of the Victorian poet, Matthew Arnold, author of *Dover Beach*. Unusually, for Nagra, this poem is not one that captures the dialectical colour of his Punjabi heritage (check out his reading of his poem *Darling & Me!* on his website).

At present as the UK agonises about migrants and refugees potentially draining the life force out of the country, this poem becomes even more relevant than when first published in 2004. The poem certainly will not ease such agonizing as it plays up to a certain view of economic migrants as projected by conservative, right wing politics. It is a curious poem that seems to simultaneously look inwards and outwards, not an easy feat to achieve.

## 2

**What's in a title? What's in a subtitle?**

A good way to dive into this poem is to fragment it into pieces. Group the most memorable descriptions of place; effective descriptions of reproduction and multiplication and descriptions of brazen conspicuous success. Put your class into groups and ask them to come up with a title based on the fragments they've been given. Then ask them for a subtitle. You could make it challenging for them by asking them to link it to another poem of their choice. If this was too much of a stretch you could furnish them with a few potential candidates! Maybe throw in *Dover Beach* for good measure. Now get them to look at the sets of fragments as one entire text and see what they come up with.

It is doubtful they will arrive at a title like *Look we have coming to Dover!* Typical of the duality of the poem, this title can be interpreted in two ways, resulting in quite divergent tones. Unsurprisingly, perspective is the key. If viewed through the eyes of a grammatical stickler then such an exclamation reveals ignorance and poor mastery of English. If viewed through the eyes of a migrant then such a grasp of the language allows clear communication. It may also reveal pride in the readiness for such a new life. For the reader, whom it can only be hoped is more neutral in perspective, it reveals an almost comic entry into the poem. There is something sweetly amusing about the grammatical fallings of this exciting glimpse of a new world. Regardless of perspective, what the title does is to privilege and prioritise the migrant voice. This is most definitely the voice of the outsider coming in. It is an enthused, innocent voice.

The subtitle's intertextual allusion to *Dover Beach* has a complex effect. On one level it reveals the huge excitement of what awaits these migrants as Dover and all it symbolizes comes into view; hence providing thematic support for that first eager exclamation. However, this new voice is distinctly English, an educated voice that diverges from the initial migrant voice in its precise mastery of the English language. It is the upper middle class voice of the impressive and rather serious looking fellow in the picture, Matthew Arnold. Therefore, Nagra presents a clash of voices before the poem even really begins, which introduces subtly the duality at the heart of the poem. Furthermore, the quotation from *Dover Beach* has been twisted out of its original tonal context. It comes from the end of Arnold's poem where he locates his existential pain in the discrepancy between the beauty of the world as it should be and its chaotic reality. Here Nagra suppresses the chaotic loneliness but keeps the wonder. In another way, this mimics the natural coping mechanism of any migrant travelling to a new, potentially unwelcoming place: stay positive, ignore any negatives!

## 3
### Welcome to the new old familiar world: sensory overload

Nagra's poem is a sensory barrage for migrant and reader. Unsurprisingly, the first two stanzas are the most sensually overwhelming, with visual, auditory, tactile as well as olfactory imagery. This overload is skilfully twisted to create a hostile physical environment; a development that undermines the chirpy naivety of the poem's title. It is notable how the migrants 'stowed' away on board are confronted with the 'lash of a diesel-breeze'. Here the aggressive onomatopoeia of 'lash' overwhelms the gentle connotations of 'breeze'. Not only does this tactile image suggest hostility in the natural environment to their arrival it also creates uncomfortable connotations with whips, slaves and masters. Furthermore, Nagra uses sibilance that mimics the sound of the sea and the 'lash' of the wind: 'stowed in the sea to invade / the alfresco lash.' While Britain's colonial past is summoned cleverly in this image, it also heightens the sensory assault through the olfactory queasiness of a 'diesel-breeze'.

This queasiness is further developed through the 'ratcheting speed into the tide', where the physical movement of the boat through the sea is clearly not designed for migrant comfort. Furthermore, in a symbolic sequence the migrants are literally assailed by the 'surf'. However, this tactile imagery is complicated by the language used. The migrants are besieged by 'gobfuls of surf phlegmed' by rich tourists 'lording the ministered waves'. The position of these 'cushy come-and-go' types is predictably at the front of the boat. Nagra puns nicely on this by describing them as 'prow'd' allowing an unpleasant vanity to characterize these rich people. More worryingly, the conflation of the sea and the rich passengers suggests that the potential xenophobia the migrants might face on the mainland is widespread.

This negative feeling is enhanced in the second stanza where a new sense is introduced: sound. Two significant sounds animate this stanza as the excitement of the initial glimpse of the cliffs gives way to something much more anxiety inducing. The seagulls bring an auditory element to the sensory assault faced by the migrants. Nagra describes them as 'vexing their blarnies'. The verb 'vexing' signals an angry tone and the noun 'blarnies' alludes to the incomprehensibility of the natives they will soon encounter. The symbolism of the 'thunder' adds a further note of menace to their impending arrival. The fact that it 'unbladders /yobbish rain and wind' down on them symbolically prepares them for the storm of indigenous reaction that may await them. The storm literally pisses down on top of them and the adjective 'yobbish' possesses depressing connotations of skinheads and BNP or National Front fanatics. It is no surprise then that the glowing white cliffs first sighted, symbolising hope and new beginnings, have now become a 'vast crumble of scummed/cliffs'. Naive enthusiasm is being squashed by harsh reality.

**4**

### Presentation of the newcomers: pestilence to residents

This emphasis on the potentially volatile and violent reaction to their arrival is achieved cleverly by blurring perspectives. While the poem is clearly from the perspective of the migrant [look at the various first person pronouns 'I' and 'we'] the language used to describe them is most definitely not language they would use themselves. Rather it is the language of the native, who spies a potentially troublesome newcomer.

This first indication of uneasiness begins when their arrival is described by the verb 'invade'. This military term connotes both an unwanted arrival as well as an inevitable cultural conflict. Other verbs are similarly revealing: The verb 'stowed' conjures up ideas of stowaways, figures who should not be travelling but who ultimately are. In the second stanza, not only does the British sky literally piss down on them they are described as 'hutched in a Bedford van'; the unusual verb 'hutched' is associated with the storage of rabbits and suggests that not only are the migrants animalistic, they are also highly reproductive.

Anxiety about unwanted cultural aliens is played upon expertly by Nagra for the remainder of the poem. This hyperproductivity of rabbits is developed further in the third stanza where the migrants lurking in our midst are 'teemed for breathing', a phrase that puns cleverly to suggest 'teamed for breeding' – every xenophobe's worst nightmare! Not only do they seem to be as plentiful as the 'sweeps of grass' in the park, their power is visualized in their 'poling sparks from pylon to pylon', a striking image that sees the migrants infiltrate the very energy systems of the country. Worryingly, this implies a parasitic strengthening at the expense of the indigenous population. Look at the extended horticultural conceit of grafting in the fourth stanza, where 'swarms' of migrants graft themselves unnoticed onto the host nation, eventually gaining the strength to move 'barefaced' into 'the clear'. The adjective 'barefaced' connotes arrogance, which carries with it the appalled indignation of the white Little Englander. The language used in these stanzas suggests an infestation spreading unnoticed under our noses, one that will only make itself known when it cannot be reversed.

The dominance of visual imagery is surely no coincidence in the final stanza. The migrants transition from hiding in 'the black', 'unclocked by the national eye', to boldly instructing the reader to 'imagine' them luxuriating in wealth. There is a provocative tone of antagonism in the description of the migrants 'Blair'd in cash' where they are 'free' from restraint in their conspicuous enjoyment of wealth. Again Nagra's punning suggests a loud, conspicuous enjoyment of their success through 'Blair'd' echoing 'blared'. The image of these self-made migrants toasting both their own success and their cultural origins in the 'East' can be read as a condemnation or as a celebration. I assume that it is a celebration, but it is elastic enough to recognize a contrary response and allow both to exist side by side.

## 5

### Speaking in foreign: noise in the poem

A final auditory image of 'babbling … lingoes' reconnects with the 'vexed blarnies' of the second stanza. But, significantly, in this case it is the migrants who make the noise rather than having to listen to it. Ultimately, Nagra ends his poem with a powerful visual image of the migrants 'flecked by the chalk of Britannia!' A mixing of cultures is signalled, but one where their original Indian heritage is very much in the ascendant. The fricative harshness of being 'flecked by the chalk of Britannia' implies that this is not a harmonious process; rather it is a state reached through tribulation, through cultural conflict. The sharp fricative of the –ck further enhances the unsettling

moment of their cultural revelation. Could it be that the triumphant, almost boastful, success of the migrants at the end of the poem has been learned from the self-assumed superiority of their ex-colonial overlords? It would be tempting to think so, an irony that would no doubt be lost on Little Englanders.

While auditory imagery is a way of illustrating the journey from silent, enduring anxiety to a more confident self-actualisation, the words of the poem itself are also rich in their sound patterns. For example, the memorable alliteration of the moment when the migrants step confidently into the open is located in the last line of the penultimate stanza; they are now 'human' enough to 'hoick' themselves 'bare-faced' into the clear. Again this suggests they weren't human prior to this, according with the animalistic language used to describe them previously. The verb 'hoick' connects to the grafting/growing conceit in the stanza but can also mean to spit, which is much more provocative. Combined with the strong assonantal spondee of 'bare-faced' this is a sonically powerful moment in the poem, thus reflecting the important evolution in the migrants' cultural self-confidence. Each stanza has its own distinctive sound patterning yet the most important aspect of Nagra's carefully constructed soundscape is that his sound patterns are most pronounced in the final stanza – where the migrants are finally brave enough to find their own voice.

## 6

### Poetic pace

'Look...!' is a poem virtually tripping over itself in its early stages. The first three stanzas are characterized by a quick poetic pace where enjambment abounds. The first two stanzas essentially have enjambment in every line. A hectic, breathless pace is thus created that is countered by the sensual overload of the description. This makes sense as it mimics the struggle to take in every sensual detail of the new world of Britain in the rush of arrival. Combined with the form, which makes each stanza a sand-alone unit [note the emphatic full stop!], the first two stanzas specifically record the physicality of the place which will now be home. Each stanza almost represents one huge intake of breath followed by a frantic recounting of the barrage of sensory experience confronting these long travelling migrants.

However, this sense of excited observation begins to slow towards the end of the poem. The final stanza only has two examples of enjambment, which imposes a more stately pace. In the context of the overall narrative trajectory of the poem this is apposite; the migrants have now established themselves in their new home. Now 'Blair'd in cash' they are confident and conspicuous as they emerge from their initial anxious desires to blend into the background, hiding 'in / the black within shot of the moon's / spotlight'.

## 7
### Form

Nagra has shaped his poem into five regular looking five line stanzas, or cinquains. Roughly speaking, his stanzas have a short opening line [5 to 7 syllables] followed by three longer lines [mostly 10 to 12 syllables] and a final line, which is the longest [14 or 15 syllables]. There is no rhyme scheme and the metre while full of strong beats is unpredictable and essentially free verse. So why does he impose such a visually rigid form on this unpredictable, high paced torrent of description?

While the regular rigidity of the form contrasts markedly with the irregularity of the poetic content, it is visually distinct and invites analysis. In one sense the form of the stanzas mimics the growth in numbers as well as cultural strength of the migrants. In a term favoured by alarmists there is a clear 'wave'-like aspect to the form. Each stanza looks like a wave coming closer and closer up the shore before retreating to start all over again (a device that mirrors, but adapts, the form of Arnold's *Dover Beach*). While this connects clearly to the journey by sea, it also links to the concept of cycles, in this case cycles of human migration from the developing world to the West. Another more out-there interpretation of the form provides us with five cinquains or five by five, a term used in radio communication to rate the loudness and the clarity of a radio signal. Applying this to the poem, the voice of the migrants has grown from silent anonymity to a voice that is loud and clear.

In summary, Nagra's poem plays on racist stereotyping of immigrants, using this knowingly and satirically. An innocent immigrant enthusiasm for England is confronted by the experience of xenophobic hostility and ugly weather. But the poem ends happily, at least, for the immigrants, safely prosperous.

**Come we make good crunching now!**

**STOWED – LASH – BRUNT – PHLEGMED – PROW'D – SEAGULL – BLARNIES – CRUMBLE – UNBLADDERS – HUTCHED – REAP – NATIONAL – TEEMED – SWEEPS – ENNOBLED – SWARMS – BLACK – MIRACLE – PASSPORT – BARE-FACED – IMAGINE – BLAIR'D – FREE – RAISE – LINGOES**

The innocence and experience narrative arc of _**Look we have coming to Dover!**_ links it to poems such as Copus' _**An Easy Passage**_ and Dunmore's _**To My Nine-Year-Old Self**_. The poem's setting and innovative use of form would make an interesting comparison with Burnside's _**History**_, while the theme of identity and place link Nagra's poem to Heaney's _**Out of the Bag**_ as well as Duffy's _**The Map-Woman**_. Finally, the satirical take on modern could be compared to O'Driscoll's _**Please Hold**_ or Turnbull's _**Ode to a Grayson Perry Urn**_.

# Sean O'Brien, *fantasia on a theme of James Wright*

**1**

A striking theme of this poem is that of journeying, of passage, and of time. Even within the title, we notice the idea of development and exposition; a *fantasia* is a musical term meaning a form that develops and grows within its key musical themes, often in an improvisatory style, or using mixed forms and styles. At first glance, it might not appear that the poem 'improvises' - the stanzas are all three lines long and visually the poem is neatly arranged. However, O'Brien does some very interesting things with his source material. His subject matter takes the poem from a definite location - 'West Moor and Palmersville' - right through to the wholly abstract and threatening 'newly opened darkness'.

A published critic as well as poet, O'Brien is self-conscious about how he addresses this poetic architecture. The poem takes its immortalised miners down the 'underground rivers' and winding 'tiny corridors' of the poem itself, ever deeper 'inside the earth' and, finally, into 'newly opened darkness'. The steady but relentless journey further and deeper inside the bowels of the earth reflects, in its nine stanzas, the nine circles of hell in Dante's *Inferno* (a 14th century epic poem depicting the journey of Dante through the underworld). Significantly, O'Brien published a verse version of Dante's text in 2006. As well as the nine stanzas, the miners are presented like ghosts inhabiting an underground world and the poem's use of tercets also echoes the stanza form of Dante's poem.

This theme of journey is reflected in different ways: the journey through time; the journey from near to Earth's surface 'sinking slowly further... to black pools in the bed of the world'; the journey from miners being remembered as semi-individuals to anonymity in death - 'We hardly hear of them'.

## 2
### Elegy
The *Fantasia* also has another strong literary connection, to the work of Wilfred Owen, the most famous trench poet of WWI, who wrote extensively on the futility and pity of war. There are many examples of images that seem to speak to each other across the decades:

- Owen's poem *Miners* describes 'the coals murmuring of their mine, /And moans down there /Of boys that slept wry sleep': O'Brien's says that 'The singing of the dead inside the earth /Is like the friction of great stones', an image which also appears in Owen's poem *Strange Meeting* - 'Through granites which titanic wars had groined'
- In Owen's same poem, he ends with the image of the future living- 'Comforted years will sit soft-chaired, /In rooms of amber'. Likewise, O'Brien ends with the image of 'The living will never persuade them /That matters are otherwise, history done'
- In Owen's poem *Strange Meeting*, the 'encumbered sleepers groaned, /Too fast in thought or death to be bestirred... with piteous recognition in fixed eyes, /Lifting distressful hands'. O'Brien's dead are equally

homogenous and in a state of sleeplike non-existence- 'Gargling dust, going down in good order, /Their black-braided banners aloft, /Into flooding and firedamp'.

The effect that is half-achieved is that of *prosopopeia,* which means giving voice to the dead. It is a technique used in Anglo-Saxon poetry as well as in classical literature, often to give an unfamiliar perspective on a situation. Owen does this overtly in *Strange Meeting,* with a dead soldier who speaks directly to the poem's narrator, but O'Brien gives no words to the miners. O'Brien is immortalising these men in language, a form of elegy or eulogy that, nevertheless, does not speak their names. Just as the poem finishes and is subsumed like 'water into newly opened darkness', the identities, faces and names of the miners are lost, forgotten by 'the living'. The poem seems to be suggesting that just as language is fleeting, so is memory. Even though we are built on the pasts of anonymous men and women that are 'dead inside the earth', whose pasts we cannot quite access, we all belong to a narrative that moves relentlessly on through history.

**3**

**Journey towards the past**
Like the small path beside the abyss, falling away from the world of the dead in Philip Pullman's **Northern Lights** trilogy, the reader is led delicately by the narrator on a thin path that both allows us to observe and participate in this journey towards the darkness. Vast swathes of history are walked through here - geological time spanning millions of years shrinks to the infinitesimally small 'shiftless seams' in the coalface, which then gather in 'black pools in the bed of the world'. Just as time forces us into the future, it also forces those left behind backwards, 'going down in good order', rendering the fleeting worries of this world such as 'spent economies' and meaningless and temporary.

The language, like the 'underground rivers', also ebbs and flows towards this inevitable ending. Harsh and stuttering consonants litter the opening few stanzas, like the juddering of something being pulled underground: 'guttering cap-lamps bound up in the roots', 'black pools in the bed of the world'. Dense alliteration of sounds such as repeated 'f', 's' and 'th' towards the end of the poem indicate a more slippery ending - 'a cla<u>ss</u>... immortali<u>z</u>ed by want if no<u>th</u>ing el<u>se</u>. /<u>Th</u>e <u>s</u>inging of the dead in<u>s</u>ide the ear<u>th</u> /I<u>s</u> like the <u>fr</u>iction of great <u>s</u>tone<u>s</u>, or like the ru<u>sh</u> /O<u>f</u> water into newly opened darkne<u>ss</u>'. The alliterative patterning recalls Anglo-Saxon verse, lending an ancient feel to the lines, as if we are journey inwards, downwards but also backwards in time:

'**G**argling **d**ust, **g**oing **d**own in **g**ood order'

The 'shiftless seams' of geological time, between coalfaces, are also reflected in the same shiftless seams between stanzas; only three of the nine, at beginning, middle and end, finish with a full stop. The others move onto the next stanza mid-sentence, the hiatus created in the poetic rhythm reminiscent of going down steps, of moving down a level. Barriers close the miners off again and again; they are trapped in 'the tiny corridors of the immense estate' before 'the thud of iron doors sealed once for all' commits them to the logbooks of time.

O'Brien's writing is muscular, with rich language concentrated into short, controlled stanzas. Whereas Owen's *Strange Meeting* expands into looser verse, without curtailed stanzas, this poem closely steers us through the  narrative journey, an approach that arguably makes the progression more suffocating and intimidating in its controlled, firm voice. A true fantasia form, in music, would expand the subject material into perhaps a fugue (adapting and layering the tune to make it appear in all different parts of the texture) or vary it so that it is re-iterated in different and multiple ways. O'Brien's poem forms a quickening spiral down into the abyss. The fact that the poetic voice narrates in present tense takes the reader right to the centre of the poem, carrying our 'prayers and lamentation' to a place where they cannot be found.

**4**

**The common man**

O'Brien takes as his theme James Wright, an American poet from a family of factory workers who wrote poetry inspired by the suffering and poverty he witnessed as a child, as well as the desolation caused by his time serving in Japan during the American occupation in 1946. Like Owen and like O'Brien,

his work bore witness, speaking for the 'common man' and about profound issues of political voice and social equality. The notion of the 'common man' is encapsulated in the image of a soldier. The soldier is someone who embodies a paradox - that of being free to democratically elect a government, but who might be subject to conscription and forced employment during wartime by the same people who were freely elected. By immortalising them in verse, the gift of language and speech gives the otherwise forgotten characters agency and power. However, one could argue that by giving something a name, you afford it a social position; these miners, carrying their 'black-braided banners' like an ancient army have none. Indeed, the poem's imagery connects them to natural and eternal forces - to the 'rush of water' and the 'friction' of stones.

By not specifying a single miner O'Brien allows his message to represent all those who die voicelessly. Interestingly, Owen's use of giving voice to the dead in *Strange Meeting* gives the narrator a relationship and character, by the very fact that there is an exchange of dialogue; some critics argue that the German soldier is his psychological double. Here, the narrator is alone, and the poem takes them (just the same as it takes the reader) on this journey towards 'newly opened darkness'.

An interesting image here is that of 'the tiny corridors of the immense estate' lined 'with prints of Hedley's *Coming Home.'* The painting that O'Brien refers to is actually called *Going Home* by an artist called Ralph Hedley, painted in 1889; as you can see, the image is of two miners leaving their day's work to return back home. The choice of changing title has many different implications. It seems unlikely that it would be an undeliberate mistake on O'Brien's part; instead, the change in title both reflects the warping of reality as the poem develops onwards (one might say as the poem 'goes down the rabbit hole') but also the fact that the poem pulls the miners in, so that they are *coming* towards it, not *going* home away from it. This adds to the overall effect of sucking the miners, and the reader, further into the text until it loses temporal and

geographical structure at the 'newly opened darkness'.

This also implies that there is a sort of homecoming for those miners being pulled underground. The Bible verse 'By the sweat of your brow you will eat your food until you return to the ground, since from it you were taken; for dust you are and to dust you will return' (Genesis 3:19) is as important here as it is for Pullman, who continually invokes this image. The image is not necessarily as violent here as it is in *Strange Meeting,* which claims straight away that 'I knew we stood in Hell'. Instead, O'Brien's poem lulls us towards a sense of peace and stasis, away from 'the hopelessness' of Owen. 'Prayers and lamentation' lose their words and become 'singing... inside the earth'. There is something untouchable, yet ethereal and restful, about that 'newly opened darkness'; it does not carry the same horror of that 'profound dull tunnel' in *Strange Meeting.*

**5**

**Further questions:**
Do you think O'Brien succeeds in laying these men to rest?
Do you think poetry can really offer this sort of conclusion?

97

***Fantasia on a Theme of James Wright* crunched:**

**MINERS – UNDERGROUND – COAL – SHIFTLESS – HOME – DUST – FIREDAMP – CORRIDORS – FAINT – SPENT – EXPLOSIONS – THUD – DOORS – SEALED – LAMENTATION – SINGING – DEAD – FRICTION – DARKNESS – BROTHERS – HISTORY**


A number of the poems in the Forward anthology are also elegiac, notably *On her Blindness* and *Effects*. If O'Brien's poem is read as intertextually being in dialogue with James Wright, Wilfred Owen and Dante's *Divine Comedy* then it shares some common ground with *Look we Have Coming to Dover!* and *Ode to a Grayson Perry Urn*. Its social engagement on the side of the oppressed might link *Fantasia on a Theme of James Wright* to *Giuseppe* and to *Song*.

# Ciaran O'Driscoll, *please hold*

## 1

### The scream

Norwegian artist, Edvard Munch's Expressionist painting **The Scream** is

probably the most iconic image of angst and alienation. Completed in 1883, the painting depicts an androgynous figure with a skull-like head crossing a bridge towards us, screaming. Whereas Impressionist painters tried to capture transient external reality, Expressionists sought to convey their own intense feelings, projecting these onto their canvases. Here it is as if the character's scream echoes through and is converted visually into an intense swirling landscape. Google the image and you'll see that the correspondence between screaming individual and screaming landscape is signalled by the shared colours and sinuous shapes. It's as if the entire natural world has become a scream.

What does O'Driscoll's poem have in common with Munch's painting?

In *Please Hold* the narrator experiences similar feelings of alienation and entrapment and, of course, he ends up screaming. O'Driscoll's poem dramatises a theme that is perhaps the most common in all literature and art - the often fraught relationship between the individual and society. Where the cause of the screaming in Munch's painting is not obvious, in *Please Hold*, as in some dystopian sci-fi, the trauma comes from interaction with the faceless authority of a machine.

## 2

### Untruths

Though the poem is undoubtedly comic and the situation the narrator finds himself is presented as being absurd, it has serious points too. Real human communication is here being replaced by automated systems, supposedly in the name of efficiency. But, as anyone who has ever had the misfortune of spending time locked into one of these sort of circular interactions with an automated answering machine will know too well, often the time-devouring, temper-testing experience is far from efficient. Moreover, there is a loss of proper human interaction. Though it might mimic some of the features of human conversation, such as turn-taking, this conversation is a fake. Despite all the options on offer, the interaction also fails its basic purpose; to address the narrator's actual 'needs'. Furthermore some cultural commentators, such as the radical economist Charles Eisenstein, argue that the sort of corporate lying inherent in this wearingly familiar aspect of modern life is actually damaging and dangerous. Over time universally used untruths, such as the fake friendliness of 'your call is important to us', degrade the quality of our communication and erode our ability to distinguish truth from lies, making us all more vulnerable to manipulation. Or so they argue.

## 3

### Dead language

Stylistically, with its ironic relocation of the colourless functional language of officialese into the lyric world of poetry, O'Driscoll's *Please Hold* is related to poems such as Henry Reed's WWII poem *Naming of Parts*, Peter Porter's *Your Attention Please* and Simon Armitage's *Hand Washing Technique* –

***Government Guidelines.*** In his poem, Reed ironically contrasts the stark, flat, euphemistic language of the military with sonorous imagery describing nature. As a recruit is instructed how to assemble a gun - 'this you can see is the bolt. The purpose of this/ Is to open the breech, as you see. We can slide it/ Rapidly backwards and forwards...' his mind wanders onto the beauty of nature, expressed in romantic mode:

**'The branches/ hold in the gardens their silent, eloquent gestures.'**

Porter's poem imitates the bland language of a public information broadcast; the terrifying idea of a nuclear attack and inevitable annihilation is related through unemotional and practical sounding, but hopelessly inadequate, instructions. A response to the enquiry into the apparent suicide of the arms expert and UN weapons inspector David Kelly in 2003, Armitage's poem ironically applies government advice on handwashing to this context. A **found poem**, such as Armitage's, is made of language discovered in any non-poetic context and then re-presented as a poem. While Reed's, Porter's and O'Driscoll's are not strictly found poems, they all use language as if verbatim, drawn from about the most distinctly non-poetic contexts conceivable.

The language in O'Driscoll's poem is, for example, devoid of metaphors or other types of figurative imagery, such as symbolism or personification. Nor are there any instances of the other form of imagery, sensory. Sensory imagery is evocative; it helps us to visualise, hear and feel the words of a poem, forging connections between us and the experiences described. O'Driscoll's poem is entirely stripped of sensory imagery. Mostly composed of dull, prosaic function words, the poem also features very few adjectives. The ones it does include, such as 'great' and 'wonderful' are colourless and emptied, in this context, entirely of meaning. Language can be simple, literal, pared-down and yet still beautiful. The language *in Please Hold*, however, is deliberately flat, lumpen, graceless and ugly.

Elegant variation is a writing principle that underpins a lot of stylish writing. In a nutshell it means avoiding repetition of words, phrases, syntax, punctuation

101

and sentence lengths, unless doing so serves a specific purpose. O'Driscoll artfully ignores this principle so that his poem is full of clumsy and grating repetition:

- On a word level, lots of words are repeated when synonyms could easily have been found: 'future', 'wife', 'giving', 'when', 'number', 'wonderful', 'great', 'account', 'money', 'options', 'nothing', 'says', 'please', 'hold', 'robot', 'means', 'grow' and so forth. Often they are repeated close together, sometimes in succeeding lines

- often these repeated words also appear in the same position in a line. The word 'number', for instance, appears at the end of line 8, 10, 11 and 12, whereas nine lines start with 'and'

- phrases are also repeated: 'my wife says', 'please hold', 'says the robot', 'you can say' etc.

- the phrase 'And my wife says, This is the future' is repeated like a refrain, with a number of slight variations

- groups of lines are also repeated, such as the first three. About two thirds of the way through the line 'and I'm talking to a robot on the phone' is reused, implying we have are back to start and the 'conversation' has gone precisely nowhere

- the syntax of many of the lines is strikingly similar: subject, verb, object

- many of the sentences are of a similar length

- full stops and commas litter the poem, only relieved by one set of brackets and one exclamation mark!

- typically the sentences are declaratives, statements rather than descriptions. Declarative sentence follows declarative statement with very little change or relief

- Some lines and sentences start and end in the same way, giving the impression that there has been no progress or movement. The best examples of this circularity are the poem's first three lines which start and end with 'future says...' The last stanza also opens and closes with the phrase 'Please hold'. The first thing we read, the title, *Please Hold* is also the last: The phrase preceding this 'This is the future' was also the first line. So, like the narrator, the reader has been caught up in an enormous, closed loop. Even at the end of the poem we haven't reached any conclusion or end point; the last thing we read is 'please hold'. In this way the present and the future collapse into each other and become indistinguishable in the poem; literally we are going around in circles, getting nowhere.

In neat mimicry of the laborious automated answering service, we've established that the poem is jam-packed full of clumsily, inelegantly, repetitive, dull, soulless language which loops back, entrapping itself. With all those commas and full stops, bereft of the underpinning spring of metre, it's also rhythmically ugly, choppy, lumpy and flat. The poem's lines move awkwardly, in jagged fits and starts; there is no flow or elasticity to the language, as there would be in real human conversation.

### So, what's the effect of this all-pervasive repetition?

Clearly it conveys the spirit-sapping poverty of the (mis)communication that's taking place, the degrading of real human experience. Simple language should at least make the transaction quick and simple. In fact, it does nothing of the sort, because this is not a proper two-way conversation. It also makes the reader feel what the poem's narrator feels – trapped in an inauthentic

'conversation' that is going nowhere and going there excruciatingly slowly. This is a modern sort of hell. Because, as well as the functional language of the answering machine being unpoetic, it is also blatantly insincere, and that just adds insult to the injury.

Presumably, for example, the answering machine is not in a position to judge whether the narrator's phone number is or is not 'wonderful'. As the narrator sarcastically observes 'I have a wonderful telephone number'. If it is not an evaluation of the quality of the number, the 'wonderful' most refer to the fact that the narrator has provided his number, something unlikely to be labelled as 'wonderful' by any real or sane person. The same goes for the abuse of the word 'great'. The reason for using an automated service is not, in fact, to make the experience as straightforward and painless as possible for the user, but to save the money, the cost of paying a real person to take the call. Hence phrases such as 'we appreciate your patience' and 'your call is important to us' are blatantly untrue and part of what drives the narrator into such a frenzy of impotent rage.

## 4
### Dystopia now!

O'Driscoll's poem paints a bleak picture of the present/future in which potentially rich human interactions are supplanted by human to machine ones.

Interestingly, the poet consistently refers to an automated service as a robot and as a 'he'. 'Robot' has distinctly Sci-fi connotations that automated answering service does not. In Sci-fi dystopias, such as the *Terminator* films the machines are taking over and aim to crush all human resistance. In *Please Hold* the machines do not rise up and conquer mankind with superior intelligence and high-tech weaponry. Instead this robot drives its human interlocutor to the point of distraction, wasting his life and vanquishing his spirit. Quite an effective tactic, in fact.

This is a comic poem. It presents an absurd situation: We have, for instance, a 'mind-reading robot'; when the man says he will be driven to looting, the robot's response is 'wonderful', and after the musical interlude the man discovers that the robot transfers him back to itself. And so on. Moreover, the narrator's escalating frustration and impotency, in contrast to the robot's unchanging blankness, is painfully entertaining (for us). But, as the final, separate stanza makes clear, there's a serious issue too. The poet implies that there's an element of deliberate control underlying the apparently helpful use of an automated service: 'please do what you're told'. After all, these interactions can only follow a predetermined pattern, fixed by the 'service provider'. It's not possible to get into an argument you can win with an automated service, there's no chance to complain or make a case or change the nature of the exchange. This fixedness denies the human a voice and disempowers him, reduces the narrator to passively following instructions. The robot has all the power.

What of the overall form of the poem? Apart from the final tercet it's one unremitting block of language, a wall of words against which the poet and reader can bang their heads, repeatedly.

Crunching **Please Hold** further highlights the repetitiveness of the poem's diction.

**FUTURE – SAME – PRESENT – ROBOT – OPTIONS – NEEDS – WONDERFUL – NUMBER – GREAT – NUMBER – NUMBER – NUMBER – NOTHING – TELEPHONE – REALLY – MONEY – NOTHING – FREE - SHOUT – WONDERFUL – GREAT – WONDERFUL – FUTURE – UNDERSTAND – SAY – SAY – CAN – ROBOTIC – SCREAM – FUTURE – SAME – PRESENT – ROBOT – OPTIONS – GUISE – APPRECIATE – HOLD – HOLD – FUCKING – HIMSELF – IMPORTANT – MEANS – NOT – FUTURE – HOLD – MEANS – NEEDS – LOOTING – COLD – TOLD – HOLD.**

With its comic/ serious satirical take on modern culture, **Please Hold,** could be compared with **One to a Grayson Perry Urn, From the Journal of a Disappointed Man, Chainsaw versus the Pampas Grass** and **The Map-Woman.**

# Ruth Padel, *you, Shiva, and my mum*

Before reading Padel's poem present the class with the following list of  quotations. Their task is to try to make intelligent guesses about the person being described here (age, gender, personality), his (or her) relationship to the person doing the describing and how the narrator might feel about this person.

- 'went to India.../For a week in the monsoon'
- visited 'Maa Markoma', where 'Orissa's last/ Recorded human sacrifice took place'
- 'rode a motorbike/ Pillion, up a leopard-and-leeches path/ Through a jungle at full moon'
- 'shove(d) away/ The sleeping buffalo'
- 'climbed barefoot..../Up a rock-slide' to 'where God sat'
- 'forded Cobra River/ In a hundred degrees at noon'
- 'wrestled a crocodile into submission.../vanquished a tribe of ferocious pigmy head hunters'.

My guess is that we'd assume that the character performing these feats is a fearless, indomitable adventurer either young or young-at-heart. They are also courageous, physically strong and hardy. Someone who's a bit of a daredevil, or who's like Indiana Jones, perhaps. The narrator describes these exploits with awe. The narrator seems to be amazed not only by the feats themselves but also by the fact this particular person has performed them. Perhaps some smarty-pants in the class will conjecture that as poets tend to present their subjects in an unusual way that it is most likely that this character might, in fact, be very old or frail or weak. If you do get an insufferably clever answer like this then at least you can congratulate yourself for how well you've prepped your class in how to read poetry.

In Padel's poem it is, of course, the narrator's mother who has stoically performed such an impressive array of tasks, in order to honour her son's wedding. It appears that these sort of experiences, and the way she reacts to them, are not her normal behaviour: 'she who hates all frills/ watched her feet painted', 'without a murmur', 'lifelong sceptic as she is...bowed'. We tend to think of old people as being reluctant to try new things and, certainly, to go on adventures, so these details are surprising. Certainly the poet seems incredulous that 'at the age of eighty' which is, after all, very old, her mother has shown such derring-do.

Each sentence in this poem is a question, beginning with the repeated phrase 'How she'. It's as if the narrator cannot quite believe what she's saying. In Glynn Maxwell's excellent poetry primer, *On Poetry*, he suggests readers should try to imagine where a poem might take place and how it might best be delivered. One poem might be best declaimed from a soapbox, another whispered in bed, another recited silently in one's head. What might be the natural context of Padel's poem? I think the kitchen table, or over the phone. Unmetred and unrhymed, there's a strong sense here of a voice speaking, relaying improbable details to a listening audience.

There's a marked absence of figurative, flashy or inflated language in the poem. The absence doesn't make the language plain, however. The Indian jungle setting with its associated place names, Orissa, the Cobra River and

Maa Markoma (pictured above), for instance, are all exotic. So too are animals such as buffaloes and leopards. In addition the poem features the Hindu god, Shiva. There's also a splash of references to rich, vibrant colours:

- 'a mask of yellow tumeric'
- 'painted scarlet henna'
- 'navy blue'
- 'a pinky blaze of ribbons'

Mostly the language is colloquial and conversational. In particular phrases such as 'this mother of mine', 'to shove away', 'and lifelong sceptic that she is' are informal and read like someone speaking. There's nothing inflatedly poetic either about lines such as the prosaic 'was getting married to a girl'.

Enjambment is employed pervasively, with most lines, and indeed stanzas, running into each other. In contrast there are few caesuras – the only really definite one signalling the shift in perspective in the penultimate stanzas. Such extensive use of enjambment plays a major part in generating the feel of a speaking voice, a voice that is eager to tell its story. Only five sentences are strung across the poem's first 32 lines. Enjambment generates forward momentum. Conversely, the last stanza comprises five truncated sentences. Thus the movement of the verse and of time is here slowed right down.

What can we say about the form of the poem?
The poem's composed of twelve intermittently rhyming tercets. The tercet form probably sprung to mind because of the three characters of the title. The form embodies a neat, regular pattern that contains irregularity within it. On the stanza level the form is regular and predictable, perhaps akin to the overall narrative of the mother attending her son's wedding. However, within order is considerable disorder. The lines, for example, vary widely in length. The shortest 'cross-legged, navy blue' comprises only five syllables, whereas the longest has fourteen. The unpredictability of the lines is increased by the absence of any governing metre. Similarly rhymes pop up from time to time, sometimes in pairs, sometimes in threes or fours, but there's no apparent regular or predictable pattern to them: 'face' & 'place'; 'last', 'path' & 'calf';

'buffalo' & 'between the toes'; 'henna', 'murmur', 'Shiva' & 'river'; 'Hindu' & 'how you'. To me, this unpredictability, this going its own-way-ness, seems designed to be analogous to the surprising, unpredictable behaviour of the aged mother.

What about the indenting of alternate tercets?
Every other stanza is indented and the poem has an equal number of indented and un-indented stanzas. This creates a slight forwards and backwards movement in the weave of two similar and complementary patterns. Now, a cynic might suggest there's just been a typographical error here. But let's muffle our inner cynic (for a moment) and see if we can determine a better reason for the alternate indenting pattern.

In a number of ways, the mother figure occupies an in-between or liminal state: An old woman, she acts in adventurous, ageless way; a lifelong sceptic she takes part in a religious ceremony; seemingly English she embraces Indian culture and becomes part of it through the marriage of her son. The stanza pattern suggests difference, but also similarity, change but also continuity, another analogue, perhaps, to the mother's experiences. Convinced? If not, can you come up with a better explanation?

The 'you' of the title only appears at the end of the poem in its last five lines. This begs the question why the poem isn't called **My Mum, Shiva and you.** We meet the characters in that order in the poem and it seems the mother is the main focus – well over half the stanzas describe her exploits. Shiva also has a couple of stanzas to himself and he is, indeed, a god and the one the mother is travelling on pilgrimage towards. The title indicates then that, though their entrance may be very delayed, this 'you' is actually very significant.

The final stanza draws a parallel between the mother's story and the sudden presence of this other person. Are they the poet's partner, perhaps? In which case love for the mother is replaced by a couple's love for each other. The word 'miracle', in particular, links both narratives. Why is the partner's breath a 'miracle'? Maybe because this relationship was unexpected, or its continuance was in some sort of jeopardy. The image of 'breath in my ear' is very intimate, suggesting whispered speech. This links to the repeated questions of 'shall' about the story being told, as if it is a secret that doesn't have to be shared. 'Shall I tell' also foregrounds the choices a writer makes in terms of creating an impression of a character. Other information about the mother, for instance, would create another character in the reader's mind.

Those last three words blur any distinction between the narrator and the poem's 'you'. The words could be spoken by either of them. These liminal words continue the theme of mixing and meeting, adopting and adapting the poem has explored. And this is the ultimate intimacy of voices and identities merging as if into one.

*You, Shiva and my Mum* crunched:


SHALL – EIGHTY – MONSOON – BECAUSE – MARRIED – TUMERIC –
SHRINE – ORISSA – SACRIFICE – MOTORBIKE – LEOPARD – JUNGLE –
SHOVE – BUFFALO – SACRED – HOW – SCARLET – PATTERN –
SWASTIKAS – BAREFOOT – GOD – BLUE – CAVE – IMPURE –
LEATHER – COBRA – HUNDRED – BULL – BLAZE – SCEPTIC – ALL –
BOWED – FONDLY – MIRACLE – BREATH - THEM

A meatier crunch:


EIGHTY – LEOPARD – JUNGLE - GOD – MIRACLE - BREATH

Mothers feature pervasively in this anthology: Padel's poem could be
compared to *Material, Inheritance, Effects, On her Blindness* and *Out of
the Bag* in terms of its presentation of a mother figure. The liminality links the
poem to *An Easy Passage* and *From the Journal of a Disappointed Man*,
while *The Deliverer* presents a much bleaker version of Indian culture.


**NB**

We lied about the crocodile wrestling (and the pigmy head hunters).

# George Szirtes, *song*

**1**

Why is this poem called *song* rather than *poem*? For surely, at least, as the italicization of the text suggests, this is a hybrid – a combination of song and poem – a 'soem' rather than a 'pong'! Is it only *song* because the italicized sections dominate [four stanzas out of six]? If this is the case then are we to hone in on the non-italicized section, the serious and poetic heart of the matter? The italicisation of the text also is intriguing: what are we to make of the two visually distinct types of text? Do the italics represent some sort of collective voice, with the non-italicised text representing the poetic voice? This would make sense but the form complicates this by allowing not just the quatrains but also some of the sestets to become part of the italic world.

The dedication to liberal South African politician Helen Suzman, I think, brings clarity by connecting both forms through the concept of protest. Her outsider status as a lone anti-Apartheid Jewish woman in a racist South African government comprised of Calvinist Afrikaner men immediately signals a poem that celebrates and promotes the struggle of the individual for autonomy in the face of more powerful, mainstream oppression. More than anything else, this is what makes this poem a song. The dedication also foregrounds a definite type of song: the protest song. Associated with predominantly folk singers, like Woody Guthrie and Bob Dylan and the like, it brings to mind the power of song as a transmitter of protest. It also suggests with its much wider reach how much more powerful song can be than poetry in instigating social change. Maybe Szirtes here strives to combine the seriousness of poetry with the wide-reaching and mass-communicating aspects of music. In one way it seems like a reclamation of poetry's function in older times when it was a decidedly oral art form.

## 2

**Music is the poetry of the air**

If this poem is a song, what type of song is it? As previously mentioned there is a definite protest element in that it promotes the right of the individual to protest or certainly for the individual to have a voice. However, in its curious repetition it also resembles African-American blues songs in their strategy of repetition with variation. A good example of a poetic soul mate might be Langston Hughes and his Harlem Renaissance work, such as **The Weary Blues** or even his later work like **Montage of a Dream Deferred**, where popular music forms provide the formal and sometimes lyrical scaffolding for poetry exploring cultural alienation.

This repetition is encapsulated in the bookending mono-rhymed quatrains that begin and end the poem. Here the first line of 'Nothing happens until something does' is reflected in the fourth line of 'nothing happening until something does'. This phrase seems oddly childlike, almost blindingly obvious in its sentiments, but again captures the simplicity of expression associated with pop songs. However, the phrase comes from a much more complex, paradoxical space. Szirtes takes Einstein's condensation of the laws of  physics 'nothing happens until something moves' and reformulates it accordingly. The changing of the verbs is crucial: 'Moves' becomes 'does' and, consequently, emphasis is placed on active participation rather than movement, which could suggest moving away from rather than moving onto. Szirtes' new Einsteinian maxim is varied subtly, but significantly, in the final stanza to 'nothing happening. Then something does'. The dramatic effect of the caesura would not be half as striking if the reader was not aware of the variation on the original line. There is an emphatic newfound confidence in this new formulation that was missing from the start of the poem. Masculine heavy rhymes also give the poem pop song simplicity and memorability: 'does,' 'was,' 'buzz,' 'does'. As discussed previously, the repetition of 'does' here signifies that this is very much a poem about taking action.

113

**3**

## Let's make some noise

Importantly, this active approach to change is catalysed by that other significant end-rhyme: 'buzz.' Above all else this poem is about making some noise, to borrow the talent show presenter's demand for applause. Even the soundscape of the poem sees a profusion of sibilance throughout, generating the poem's energetic buzzing. The power and energy of noise animates this poem. Indeed, noise brings transformation.

The poem creates a vibrant visual image of small children confined by 'a monstrous hall'. Now while this may seem a critique of confining education, it also has a more sinister resonance of concentration camps and the aftermath of the Second World War that catapulted Szirtes' family from Hungary to England. It would not be too far a jump to extend this to the Soviet occupation of Hungary during the Cold War. The danger of noise or speech, certainly, becomes more acute when read in the context of such oppressive regimes to individual freedom. Whatever the political possibilities of such readings, it is undeniable that strength in numbers and the courage to protest leads to change; it takes 'a lot of small hands' to 'make the air vibrate' and 'shake the wall.'

It is significant that the noise of defiant protest that the 'small hands' create is transformed into a 'tune that has been sung / time and again'. Szirtes here changes articulation by converting noise into song, primal cries of injustice into sculpted lyrics of pain. To bring this back to the context of African-American blues, Ralph Ellison describes this music 'an autobiographical chronicle of personal catastrophe expressed lyrically'. The first step to dismantling discrimination is to express the pain of personal experience and if enough people do this then 'it is possible [...] / that even Earth may be made to move'. For the powerful to help the powerless they must understand the powerless. To speak/sing in the poem is to be powerful.

Understandably, Szirtes is realistic about the machinations of power as any post-WWII refugee must be, indeed as any politically astute observer must be.

Cultural domination is the domination of cultural discourse and history is full of silenced minorities. The poem puts it rather succinctly, but brutally: to be 'hushed' is to be 'crushed'. History is written or sung by winners and in the silence there is a nothingness that cannot be negated for minority groups. However, Szirtes' poem/song not only argues that the song of protest is merely historical; the conflict and turmoil associated with protest and change is as ingrained in the universe as the foundational principles of science.

## 4
### The science of sound and the sound of science

In fact, if thought about it in the scientific light introduced earlier, noise, or sound, can only be transmitted from particle to particle; there must be both a transmitter and a receiver. Such a bipartite relationship is idealized in the poem. It is not enough for an individual to 'buzz'; said 'buzz, must be validated by another. This is as true for the microscopic life, individual to individual, as it is for the macroscopic, individual to culture, or even culture to culture. If the 'buzz' leads to the 'does' then the message is clear – be brave and be the one who initiates change. You never know who will be the 'one pale feather' who tips 'the balance' of things, but it might as well be you.

However, Szirtes' use of science is not just restricted to the metaphor of sound transfer. The poem contains other scientific metaphors, which reinforce the predominant sound comparison. The law of the lever features prominently.

Not only are the key terms of 'levers', 'fulcrums' and 'weights' mentioned specifically but they are repeated for effect. The notable internal rhyme of 'fate' and 'weight' signals the importance of this metaphor in the battle for individual and cultural validation. Szirtes uses weights to signify cultural power and puns comically, if darkly, on this in his phrase 'heavy fate'. The danger of being 'crushed' is directly proportional to the cultural power of the stakeholder. While a balancing of loads, 'levers and fulcrums' is characteristic of inanimate structures, in matters of human forces such idealism appears naive at best, foolish at worst. It surely is no coincidence that Szirtes describes the tipping of the 'balance on a sinking ship' where balance is a non-entity in a catastrophic loss. Quite at odds with scientific views of a world in balanced harmony, a world of actions and equal but opposite reactions, the poem presents a world characterised by inequality – an inequality that must be consistently attacked so as to achieve equality. Of course, one man's equality is another man's inequality; it is not scientifically objective but very much a subjective concept. Balance at best is strictly temporary according to Szirtes.

According to Science, energy may neither be created nor destroyed; it can only be altered. In the poem Szirtes uses this principle to assert that social energies have the potential to be redistributed rather than created/destroyed. The law of the lever is crucial in the poem's science-inflected world as 'the object however great [...] / may be made to move.' The alliteration of the m's here makes this a memorable moment in the poem [pardon my own unintentional m-fuelled alliteration]. The image of 'one pale feather' being the thing that tips 'the balance' proposes that it only take a single individual to initiate social upheaval and rebalancing. The metaphor of the 'sinking ship' also illustrates that one society must be destroyed to create another, hopefully improves, one. In this way, this image of the feather subtly transmits a

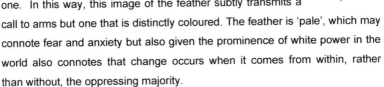

call to arms but one that is distinctly coloured. The feather is 'pale', which may connote fear and anxiety but also given the prominence of white power in the world also connotes that change occurs when it comes from within, rather than without, the oppressing majority.

This feeling of a unique moment of change is further reinforced by the beautiful weight-related simile at the end of the penultimate stanza. Here 'the heart like a weight begins to lift,' which sees a lifting off not only of oppression but also of the emotional devastation that accompanies such oppression. To equate the 'weight' with the 'heart' imaginatively describes the processes at the heart of such social change. For cultural acceptance to occur the both the oppressed and oppressor much be humanized; they must be recognized as having 'a heart' and a shared humanity promoted in cultural discourse, as

116

opposed to dehumanizing difference.

## 5

### 'Poetic form as an act of courage'

This process of social change through a recognition of shared humanity is reflected in Szirtes' chosen rhyme scheme in his sestets. The ABABCC rhyme scheme signifies the social change that the poem desires with two separate entities segregated through the crossrhyme becoming altered yet equal through the couplet at the end of the sestets. The sestets then reflect this utopian ideal for cultural equality, power-sharing and ownership.

However, what of the booming masculine mono-rhymes of the bookending quatrains? Are they barriers to such processes of social change? They certainly do not suggest change; in the fact that they are the same rhyme words and the same sound, essentially. They endow the poem with a circularity that may be viewed as confining or entrapping. However, it may be more useful to look at the poem in terms of symmetry - as being a reflection of two halves. The two halves are very similar but not exactly symmetrical, which indicates subtle changing that embodies the notion that small changes accumulate over time to initiate substantial change. Such an observation is, however, belied by the momentous forces of change that are described in the poem.

Szirtes is a great fan of the poetic devices of metre, form and rhyme and has stated that poetic form is 'an act of courage and grace, the wheeling of the skater on the ice, the tightrope walker juggling over Niagara, the builder of frail bridges across dark spaces who is not so very different from the spider spinning a web (a structured web, mind you) from his own body'. The emphasis on 'frail bridges' suggests that it might be unfair to expect every single aspect of his form to all point in the same overall direction. Indeed, this would be at odds to the poem's message of different voices singing different songs in the same culture. However, one final way of looking at these problematic quatrains is to inspect their metrical patterns. Each line is nine syllables in length and three out of the four lines contains five beats i.e.

**Noth** ing **happ** ens un **til some** thing **does**
**Eve** ry **thing** re **mains just** as it **was**
And **all** you **hear** is the **dis** tant **buzz**
Of **noth** ing **happe** ning **till some** thing **does**.

Despite the regularity of the line-lengths, the strong mono-rhymes and the quatrain form, the metrical patterns suggest the type of instability and unpredictability that instigates social change. There is a suitable unpredictability to the clustering of beats in spondees and the hypermetrical stress of the 5-beat lines, which makes the form frail in the right way. This hypermetrical loading of the lines also endows a pent-up nature to the poetic lines, almost as if they are bursting with too much energy and must be relieved. It conjures up the volatile environments that always precipitate social upheaval and so seem appropriate to the poem's content in their combustibility. Additionally, too rigid a metrical pattern would signal an oppressiveness that is contrary to the poem's message. The chosen form is still powerful, but also fluid, more suited to the poem's hopeful message about the possibility, even the inevitability of change.

**Crunch Time**

NOTHING – REMAINS – BUZZ – SOMETHING – HANDS – VIBRATE – SHAKE – BREAK – TIP – BALANCE – TUNE – AGAIN – FATE – OPPOSE – WEIGHT – HUSHED – PEOPLE – LEVER – SMALL – OBJECT – POSSIBLE – MOVE – HAPPENS – HANDS – FILL – BROKEN – SHIFT – LIFT – NOTHING – EVERYTHING – BUZZ – DOES

**A crunchier crunch:**

NOTHING – SHAKE – FATE – POSSIBLE – LIFT – DOES

***The Deliverer*** is another poem that mounts a protest against social injustice and a number of other poems in the Edexcel selection explore the subject of change, including *The Map-Woman*, *To My Nine-Year-Old Self* and *Genetics,* the last of which would also make an interesting comparison in terms of the poets' use of form. The hope *Song* articulates could also be compared to that found in *A Minor Role.* The struggle that ethnic/cultural minorities face in striving for their own authentic voice and validation can also be seen in *Look, We Have Coming to Dover!*

# Adam Thorpe, *on her blindness*

**1**

When is chopped up prose just chopped up prose and when can it be seen to clamber to the airy heights of poetry? It's a tough call for sure and novelist Adam Thorpe sails close to the wind with this free verse poem that seems to rather arbitrarily cut 17 sentences into 22 couplets and one poetically lonely line. Additionally, it also seems more like a mini-prose narrative with its collection of anecdotal observations and corresponding personal contemplations. Can clever lineation alone lift carefully arranged prose into poetry? I'm doubtful. There must be an intensity of expression, a boldness of imaginative description and a deep core of emotional profundity that rescues poetry from being merely prosaic.

Luckily, Thorpe explores loss at the uncomfortably close distance of 'a fortnight back'. Above all else it is the lack of emotional distance from the traumatic event the poem narrates that transforms his prose into poetry. Deeply personal, and consequently deeply universal, the loss of a parent awaits us all. Like the majority of such losses, the loss here is not a serene death due to natural circumstances during sleep, but a long drawn out process of deterioration, defiance and dependence.

Comprising 22 regular couplets, superficially the poem seems composed, neat and orderly. Beneath this outer composure, however, is a striking internal disorder. The regular holding outer pattern of the couplet is, in fact, under considerable internal stress. Unmetred, the form is like cut-up prose, especially in the proliferation of enjambment that characterises almost every couplet and the inevitably high number of caesuras that such enjambment creates. A combination of fast pace and stuttering pauses adds to an impression of underlying emotional turmoil. Notice how the poignancy of the ending is amplified by the loss of a poetic line in what should be the concluding couplet, a loss that mirrors the actual loss of Thorpe's mother.

## 2

### The blind leading the not-blind

*On Her Blindness* through its title reaches backwards through time to John Milton's *When I Consider How My Light Is Spent (On His Blindness)* a poem that voices the helplessness of the blind from the perspective of the blind. Crucially, Thorpe changes this perspective to those who watch the blind from the outside, who spectate on their helplessness. In an odd way this intensifies the feelings of helplessness that drive the poem. It is the contrast between the 'inadequate [...] locked-in son' and the woman who somehow 'kept her dignity' that is so striking.

It is the mother's active, stoical defiance of her 'catastrophic / handicap' that the poem promotes. Thorpe employs an almost black humour in his capturing of her plight. She is described 'bumping into cars like a dodgem', she insists

on driving 'the old Lanchester /long after it was safe' and perhaps most pathetically, she 'admires' films and television /while looking the wrong way.' There is something noble about how 'she pretended to ignore /the void; or laughed it off.' Indeed, the overall poetic message seems to advocate a healthy dose of humour in warding off the annihilating darkness of her disability. However, this is not to say that Thorpe does not treat his subject with the seriousness it deserves. He employs a molussus [and ear hooking alliteration] at the start of the 'long /slow slide had finished in a vision /as blank as stone,' which endows his topic with a befitting sonic gravity. The poet also combines this metrical power with his most effective piece of figurative language to ensure that the deft balance of tragic-comedy stays firmly in tragic waters. The 'blank as stone' simile foregrounds the dehumanising debilitation of his mother's illness and also its complete invincibility. The simile also captures something of the calcifying processes that turn her from the 'bumping [...] dodgem' to 'too weak

121

to move'.

In contrast, the poet's own passivity and powerlessness renders him more pathetic than the mother who tells him frankly she 'could not bear being blind' (one of the most memorably alliterative moments in the poem). Whereas the pretence she develops in public seems admirable in its usage as a coping strategy, his inability to say nothing or nothing of use renders him impotent, an unwilling spectator in an unwanted theatre of cruelty. His mortifying faux pas of raving about 'the autumn trees around the hospital /ablaze with colour' to his blind dying mother is searingly honest and again, darkly comic. Such awkward moments capture the reality of how 'inadequate' non-sufferers actually are for those who suffer illnesses that strip away taken-for-granted humanity.

## 3

### Seeing is pretending
However, the poem, while ending in a poignant finality, offers a shred (and I think it could only be that) of hope. The gift for pretence has been bequeathed from the dead to the living. Now, rather than his mother pretending it is 'up to us to believe /she was watching, somewhere, in the end'. In the same way that his mother memorably pretended to like his kids' 'latest drawing, or [...] new toy' as a way of making every day bearable, her mourners are encouraged to pretend to see her in a new light, to bear the burden of her loss. The poem attempts to understand the anguish of the 'living hell' his mother felt in a way that is naive, yet cathartic.

The pretending is signalled by the key verb 'believe', which gives this pretence a distinctly religious tone. To believe that the dearly departed are 'watching, somewhere, in the end' suggests a belief in an afterlife where Thorpe's mother is restored to her full powers. The caesuras surrounding 'somewhere' in the final line alter its potential meaning from 'she was watching somewhere' in the distance (i.e. gazing serenely into the distance) to 'she was watching somewhere' different (i.e. she is watching us from a different place). There is also the comic possibility, which would be disrespectful if not for the aforementioned comic treatment of his mother's disability, of her finally allowed 'to sink into television /while looking the [right] way'. Regardless, this emphasis on pretence as a coping strategy places the emphasis on the coping part rather than the pretence part. Religious beliefs can be dismissed as misguided, naive self-delusion by atheists, but should also be recognised as an imaginative coping strategy for the harshness of life; a coping method no less imaginative or consoling than the best literature has to offer.

## 4

### Afterglow or aftermath?

Hopefully, it is now apparent how conflicted this poem is in its treatment of its chosen topic – it constantly teeters on the brink of collapse, somehow traversing the boundaries between poetry and prose, tragedy and comedy, order and disorder, the trivial and the profound in a memorably awkward yet admirable manner.

 Nowhere is this more painfully acute than in Thorpe's beautiful evocation of his mother's death, nestled symbolically in the bosom of nature's beauty – a beauty that is absolutely of no consolation to his blind mother. There is something moving about the idealised 'autumn trees around the hospital /ablaze with colour' that brings so much consolation to him rather than his mother. Again, the dark comedy of his vibrant evocation of nature's beauty for his blind mother being both futile and noble embodies the crux of the problem: how do you pretend to understand something you have not experienced yourself?

Again, it seems that success in this regard is ultimately irrelevant – it is the trying to console that is more important; generosity of spirit to at least try to empathise can be enough in itself. Regardless, the setting of 'the ground royal /with leaf-fall' bestows a dignity on his mother's death that is appropriate for a woman who 'kept her dignity'. How much of an artistic pretence this is remains to be seen, but it is fitting that she departs into the metaphorical darkness 'ablaze with colour'. It reflects the vibrant strategies of affectation that his mother employed so effectively.

*On Her Blindness* crunched

**BLIND – SHOULDN'T – CATASTROPHIC – HANDICAPS – BEAR – JOY – FIGHT – RESTAURANT – FORK – TRY – WHISPERED – HELL – HOPE – RECALL – SOP – INADEQUATE – DIGNITY – DODGEM – DIRECTION – COMPASS – PRETENDED – LAUGHED – COULDN'T – SHOW – FORGET – SLIDE – BLANK – DRIVE – SAFE – EXHIBITIONS – SINK – WRONG – LAST – GOLDEN – AUTUMN – ABLAZE – LEAF-FALL – STARING – NOTHING – DYING – SIGHTLESS - EYELIDS – COFFIN – WATCHING**

A number of poems in the selection explore relationships with mothers and with mortality. Most obviously *Effects*, like ***On Her Blindness,*** is an elegy exploring both topics together. *Material*, *Out of the Bag*, *Genetics and You*, *Shiva, and my Mum* also spring to mind as potential comparisons.

# Tim Turnbull, *ode on a Grayson Perry urn*

## 1

An interesting way into Turnbull's poem would be to google Grayson Perry's

art and, in particular, the images from his exhibition *The Vanity of Small Things*. In this exhibition, artist and documentary film-maker, Grayson Perry, presents six tapestries depicting the life of a fictional character, Tim Rakewell. Starting with his birth, these intensely brightly coloured, cartoonishly rendered tapestries trace Rakewell's ascent through and across modern Britain, from the Cotswolds to Sunderland. In this way, they present a cross section of modern British culture. Characteristically, Perry's tapestries are intertextual: as titles such as *The Annunciation of the Virgin Deal* indicate, each tapestry draws on and references iconography from famous religious paintings. Echoing the series of paintings by the eighteenth century English artist William Hogarth called *A Rake's Progress*, the narrative of Rakewell is also intertextual. And, the medium itself, tapestry, sets up a series of expectations in terms of content that Perry references and subverts.

In simultaneous dialogue with John Keats's seminal poem *Ode to a Grecian Urn* (1819) and Perry's art works, Turnbull's poem follows a similarly self-consciously intertextual pattern. And, like Perry's work, Turnbull's poem uses Keats' Ode as an ironic backdrop for a vibrant but garish vision of modern

British life. As the poem states, whether this vision is celebratory or condemnatory depends on the eye of the beholder.

John Keats was part of the Romantic movement in poetry, which also included poets such as Wordsworth, Byron and Shelley. The Romantics' poetry is characterised by discussion of nature, and of the palpable sadness at man's inability to reach a true essence of purity and 'oneness' with it. Keats was credited with the reworking of the ode form (a classical Greek poem structure), and similarly, Turnbull makes no apologies for taking Keats' poem and crafting a challenging response.

Keats' poem is a tribute to, and celebration of, classical Greek art- specifically, here, an 'urn' or large vase, upon which pictures are drawn of pastoral Greek life. Keats believed that classical art presented the ideal of Greek virtue and classical life, which is the foundation of the poem. The two scenes that he chooses to narrate are a lover who fruitlessly pursues his beloved, and of some rural villagers in the lead-up to performing a sacrifice. The poem makes an implied contrast between the ideal it depicts and the contemporary world in which Keats lived.

Both poems are about the physicality of 'things', whether this be a neo-classical vase representing antique craft or 'A kitschy vase / some Shirley Temple manqué has knocked out'. Turnbull's dismissive, irreverent description of a mass-produced vase contrasts with Keats' admiration of his elegant, ancient Greek version. What do you think Turnbull is saying by setting up this comparison?

## 2

### Owed to the ode; adaptation

The most obvious piece of aesthetic, or self-aware 'creation' and artificiality, is in the title. Writers, to some extent, are always adapting previous sources (this goes right down to the very fact that all language must be re-used unless you make up your own words!) However, Turnbull might as well just cite Keats on this; he is deliberately asking the reader to examine what adaptation is and what effect it has on us. Do you think that a direct adaptation makes the writer less legitimate? Is the end work still as accomplished or do you think a writer should be coming up with as new material as possible each time? Why?

Frances Spalding noted an interesting aspect of adaptation whilst talking about Myfanwy Piper's study of Picasso – that '[Picasso's] modernity lay not in the shattering of form, but in the need to find a way of dealing with the remaining fragments... not a new world but the old world in new and shattered circumstances'. Turnbull's poem is in critical dialogue with Keats's and these 'shattered circumstances' are clearly recognisable:

- Keats' question 'What men or gods are these?... What wild ecstasy?' is answered with Turnbull's 'children. They will stay out late /forever, pumped on youth and ecstasy, /on alloy, bass and arrogance'
- Keats' sylvan 'pipes and timbrels' and 'soft pipes' become Turnbull's 'screech of tyres and the nervous squeals /of girls'
- Perhaps one of the most direct nods - after the title - that Turnbull makes to the form of Keats' poem is the ending. Whilst Keats' famous closing lines read 'Beauty is truth, truth beauty,- that is all /Ye know on earth, and all ye need to know', Turnbull suggests that, actually, reality is far more fluid and uncertain - 'who knew that truth was all negotiable /and beauty in the gift of the beholder'. Keats's lofty, declarative aphorism is replaced, and undercut, with a relativistic question, couched in everyday speech.

This is also a nod to the construction of the poem itself. The idea that the canon (the types of literature considered important and 'set in stone' for, for example, a syllabus) must be untouched is directly challenged here. The Romantic poets spent a lot of time thinking about the pure essence of beauty, especially that found in nature, and one argument for the power of their poetry is the constant sadness and distress it evokes from the fact that that pure beauty can never be attained. Perhaps Turnbull is saying that the beauty of Keats' 'original' is in his power - and that it is our gift, as a reader, to be the 'beholder' and make the poem our own. Whilst this doesn't necessarily mean we have to go out and rewrite every classical poem we come across, it does mean that no meaning is fixed - just as Turnbull has reworked a Romantic narrative voice for a modern social context. Hence Turnbull's poem reflects shifts in the concept of the reader in modern literary criticism: Whereas in Keats' time, the writer was seen as the prime controller of meaning, modern criticism, as you'll know from your A-level assessment objectives, argues that the reader is a significant, active maker of meaning. Every reading is, in effect, an act of recreation.

## 3
### How Romantic are both poems?
The Romantic period is sometimes stereotyped as being about the tempestuous lives of a group of troubled poets. This isn't really an unfair judgement as there was plenty of relationship distress amongst the poets we mentioned earlier. However, there are obviously other very important hallmarks. In particular, there was a major emphasis on the physical experience of nature and of God. Sometimes this was shown in poems like *The Eolian Harp* (Coleridge's study of a harp as a method of attaining a purity of natural experience) and sometimes it was expressed through the violence of physical creation and disorder (a perfect example being Mary Shelley's novel *Frankenstein*, written in 1818).

Turnbull also mirrors this Romantic inclination to connect with the deepest essence of human existence; he does so by bringing out the earthiest and most guttural parts of physicality and sexuality. His language evokes this earthiness all the way through. For example, the growly onomatopoeia of 'throaty turbo roar' reverberates through to 'joyful throb', to 'alloy, bass and arrogance'. The momentum of these 'o' sounds is suddenly stopped with the bright, lighter, but still harsh, 'screech of tyres and the nervous squeals / of girls'. The people 'pumped on youth and ecstasy' even enter their bodies into the horrific sounding 'chlamydia roulette'. It is worth unpicking this striking image: Karl Marx once said that women's bodies were the original form of currency as they were traded for other goods. If it were just money being gambled, we could accuse the characters of superficiality. Instead, bodies are being exchanged in an anarchic marketplace of 'lives so free and bountiful', where everything is 'negotiable' - returning to what Marx claims is the original form of currency, back to the physical roots of all human commerce.

## 4

### Free bodies

It is obviously also not just women, here, who are being traded. Each girl is 'buff [and] each geezer toned and strong'. Modern British society is depicted

in free-wheeling, vivid, Perry-style technicolour, but the vision is hardly utopian - 'given head /in crude games', 'dead suburban streets', 'rat-boys' and 'crap estates'. Perhaps we should read the poem as a lament for the cheapening and coarsening of popular culture. Indeed the poem's breezy, colloquial and sometimes coarse idiom - 'knocked out', 'pumped on', 'geezer(s)', 'given head' - stands in stark contrast to Keats' rarefied vocabulary and phrasing. Perhaps, in fact, Turnbull's poem presents a dystopian vision of societal decline.

However, the imagery is as vibrant as it is garish. And just as Keats describes the 'wild ecstasy' of the ancient Greeks, Turnbull also offers a picture of liberation - 'lives so free and bountiful', 'how happy'. Moreover, Turnbull's poem presents a world more liberal and progressive than Keats', one where the connection with our physical existence is far more accessible than the Romantics thought it was. Whereas Keats' 'heart high-sorrowful' yearns for 'all breathing human passion far above', Turnbull's 'human passion' is immediate, touchable, real.

The characters consensually engage in this world within Turnbull's text, unlike the 'heifer lowing at the skies' that is lead to the sacrificial altar in Keats' *Grecian Urn*. Another example of freedom shown in Turnbull's poem is the fact that most lines are not given a hiatus by punctuation; the majority flow freely into the next, with uncapitalised words at the beginnings of lines:

**'but these wheels will not lose traction, skid and flip, no harm / befall these children'.**

Conversely, Keats' lines are held back by constant commas, question marks and full stops, reigning the passage of language in to mirror the constrained artifice of the urn itself: 'by river or sea shore, / Or mountain-built with peaceful citadel, / Is emptied of this folk, this pious morn? / And...' These lines move hesitantly, sedately, conveying pensive thought, but also uncertainty. In stark contrast, Turnbull's ode is speeded-up, turbo-charged, at full-throttle; the lines rush onwards conveying the pace and energy of modern life.

A useful bit of philosophy to look at here is Thomas Hobbes' **Leviathan**, published in 1651. Hobbes suggested that human beings are just physical objects, and that all of their actions can be explained in purely mechanical terms. Hobbes also says that power only exists where there is a mutual agreement between the ruler and those being ruled, and perhaps most famously that all the different bodies acting in their own interests produce a world where life is 'solitary, poor, nasty, brutish and short'. We have already seen that Turnbull's characters enter their bodies as objects into the narrative's 'roulette'; the poem gives them a short life cycle before catapulting  far into the future, 'millennia hence'. They don't seem to recognise any higher authority, 'too young to quite appreciate / the peril they are in'. Life in this poem certainly seems 'short' and perhaps 'brutish'- but is it really 'nasty' or 'poor'?

Similarly, in terms of the self-reflective debate about the value of art, the poem raises the question of whether something that is variously described as 'kitschy', 'gaudy' and a 'garish crock' (phrases that could be levelled against the poem itself – the elegant, classical form of the Ode stuffed full with gaudy content) can, in fact, be just as beautiful and 'true' as great works from the literary and artistic canons.

## 5

**Further questions:**

Does Turnbull's poem reassure you that life is in front of the reader to be grasped - or does it alienate you with the intensity of description?
How far do you think both poems exaggerate or bend the truth?
Why might they do that?

*Ode to a Grayson Perry Urn* crunched

KISTCHY – VASE – KIDS – CARS – BEDLAM – FRIGHT – EXPOSE – TURBO – THROB – SQUEALS – YOUTH – ECSTASY – ARROGANCE – URBAN – GIRL – GEEZER – CHLAMYDIA – CHEERLEADERS – PENSIONERS – RICH – GARISH – FREE – HAPPY – TRUTH – BEAUTY

Turnbull emphasises the power involved throughout the process of adaptation. Other poems in the anthology that are in 'dialogue with' other poems, or artworks, include *Fantasia on a Theme of James Wright*, *Look We Have Coming to Dover!*, *On Her Blindness* and *Balaclava*. *Please Hold* is another poem which takes a comic, satirical approach to presenting modern life.

*I have a dark and dreadful secret. I write poetry.*

Stephen Fry

# Another sonnet of revision activities

1. Reverse millionaire: 10,000 points if students can guess the poem just from one word from it. You can vary the difficulty as much as you like. For example, 'incubation', would be fairly easily identifiable as from *Out of the Bag*, whereas 'pre-tourist' would be more difficult. 1000 points if students can name the poem from a single phrase or image – 'on a king-size bed'. 100 points for a single line. How about 'flash of armaments before...'? *The War Correspondent*? No, *An Easy Passage*. 10 points for recognising the poem from a stanza. Play individually or in teams.

2. Research the poet. Find one sentence about them that you think sheds light on their poem in the anthology. Compare with your classmates.

3. Write a cento based on one or more of the poems. A cento is a poem constructed from lines from other poems. Difficult, creative, but also fun, perhaps.

4. Read 3 or 4 other poems by one of the poets. Write a pastiche. See if classmates can recognise the poet you're imitating.

5. Write the introduction for a critical guide on the poems aimed at next year's yr. 12 class.

6. Practice comparing and contrasting: Write the name of each poem on a separate card. Turn face down and mix up the cards. Turn back over any three cards at random. What do two of the poems have in common? How is the third one different? Replace the cards and do the exercise again.

7. Use the poet Glynn Maxwell's typology of poems to arrange the poems into different groups. In his excellent book, *On Poetry*, Maxwell

suggests poems have four dominant aspects, which he calls solar, lunar, musical and visual. A solar poem hits home, is immediately striking. A lunar poem, by contrast, is more mysterious and might not give up its meanings so easily. Ideally a lunar poem will haunt your imagination. Written mainly for the ear, a musical poem focuses on the sounds of language, rather than the meanings. Think of Lewis Carrol's *Jabberwocky*. A visual poem is self-conscious about how it looks to the eye. Concrete poems are the ultimate visual poems. According to Maxwell the very best poems are strong in each dimension. Try applying this test to each poem. Which ones come out on top?

8. Maxwell also recommends conceptualising the context in which the words of the poem are created or spoken. Which poems would suit being read around a camp fire? Which would be better declaimed from the top of a tall building? Which might you imagine on a stage? Which ones are more like conversation overheard? Which are the easiest and which the most difficult to place?

9. Mr Maxwell is a fund of interesting ideas. He suggests all poems dramatise a battle between the forces of whiteness and blackness, nothingness and somethingness, sound and silence, life and death. In each poem what is the dynamic between whiteness and blackness? Which appears to have the upper hand?

10. Maxwell argues too that the whiteness is a different thing for different poems. Consider each poem's whiteness in the light of this idea. See any differences?

11. Still thinking in terms of evaluation, consider the winnowing effect of time. Which of these poems do you think might be still read in 20, a 100 or 200 years? Why?

12. Give yourself only the first and last line of one of the poems. Without peeking at the original, try to fill in the middle. Easy level: write in

prose. Expert level: attempt verse.

13. According to Russian Formalist critics poetry performs a 'controlled explosion on ordinary language'. What evidence can you find in this selection of controlled linguistic detonations?

14. A famous musician once said that though he wasn't the best at playing all the notes, nobody played the silences better. In Japanese garden water features the sound of a water drop is designed to make us notice the silence around it. Try reading one of the poems in the light of these comments, focusing on the use of white space, caesuras, punctuation – all the devices that create the silence on which the noise of the poem rests.

15. In **Notes on the Art of Poetry**, Dylan Thomas wrote that 'the best craftmanship always leaves holes and gaps in the works of the poem so that something that is not in the poem can creep, crawl, flash or thunder in'. Examine a poem in the light of this comment, looking for its holes and gaps. If you discover these, what 'creeps', 'crawls' or 'flashes' in to fill them?

16. Different types of poems conceive the purpose of poetry differently. Broadly speaking Augustan poets of the eighteenth century aimed to impress their readers with the wit of their ideas and the elegance of the expression. In contrast, Romantic poets wished to move their readers' hearts. Characteristically Victorian poets aimed to teach the readers some kind of moral principle or example. Self-involved, avant-garde Modernists weren't overly bothered about finding, never mind pleasing, a general audience. What impact do the Forward poems seek to have? Do they seek to amuse, appeal to the heart, teach us something? Are they like soliloquies – the overheard inner workings of thinking – or more like speeches or mini-plays? Try placing each poem somewhere on the following continuums. Then create a few continuums of your own. As ever, comparison with your classmates will prove illuminating.

Emotional..........................................................................intellectual

Feelings....................................................................................ideas

Internal.................................................................................external

Contemplative....................................................................rhetorical

Open.....................................................................................guarded


NB

Yes, we know. This is that rare old bird, a sixteen-line sonnet, following the example of the poet George Meredith, no less.

# Critical soundbites

In this demanding revision activity, students have to match the following excerpts from criticism to the poet whose work they describe. (Answers are at the end of this book). In an added twist for this second volume, some of the sound bites come from the poets themselves...

1. 'I love this big-eyed, Frankenstein-like imagining, and the shiver of remembered fear it brings with it.'

2. The poet's 'opulent, passionate flights of fancy are touched by myth and dream,' but their 'characters' sweaty desires, anger and laughter fully inhabit the here and now'.

3. 'I think in images and I like to write in images. That's what writing is all about – the transforming image that provides even commonplace things with another dimension.'

4. 'It doesn't matter if it's breath, blood, a drum loop, jazz syncopation, the pentameter or whatever, you gotta get a rhythm, a working rhythm.'

5. The poet, 'enjoys a reputation as a poet consistently sympathetic in' their 'observation of human lives – particularly of' their 'own family's history – as well as the rhythms of social change and the natural world'.

6. Apparently, poet x writes 'witty, markedly contemporary first-person lyrics with a pseudo-confessional edge that revel in what Elizabeth Bishop famously called 'the surrealism of the everyday'; exposing the false distinction between the ordinary and extraordinary through exploring the rich vicissitudes of human experience'.

7. 'It could be said that just as some writers use humour as an antidote to

despair' this poet 'uses humour to make expressions of anger more palatable.'

8. 'Perhaps' this poet's 'most significant poetic achievement so far...lies in his ability to deconstruct literary, cultural and social conventions in often darkly comic ways.'

9. Poet y 'populates' their 'work with solitary, outsider figures, sometimes only partly human, stranded on the borders between worlds and excluded from normal human relationships.'

10. Poet z's 'poems are full of social snapshots of England from his childhood in the 1950s onwards, but they developed increasingly a dream-like rather than documentary feel'.

11. 'I want my writing to be as clear as water. No ornate language; very few obvious tricks. I want readers to be able to see all the way down through its surfaces into the swamp. I want them to feel they're in a world they thought they knew, but which turns out to be stranger, more charged, more disturbed than they realised.'

12. 'There is the terrible vehicle of darkness That runs over us in hope. There is my hand, there are your fingers. We hang by our fingertips. We cope.'

13. 'The ultimate aim of the poet should be to touch our hearts by showing his own, and not to exhibit his learning, or his fine taste, or his skill in mimicking the notes of his predecessors.'

14. Their 'poems are beautifully controlled with a literary sophistication which does not preclude tenderness' their 'poems encompass historical imaginings and domestic scenes, and are appreciative of worldwide cultures'.

# Glossary

ALLITERATION – the repetition of consonants at the start of neighbouring words in a line

ANAPAEST - a three beat pattern of syllables, unstress, unstress, stress. E.g. 'on the moon', 'to the coast', 'anapaest'

ANTITHESIS - the use of balanced opposites

APOSTROPHE – a figure of speech addressing a person, object or idea

ASSONANCE – vowel rhyme, e.g. sod and block

BLANK VERSE – unrhymed lines of iambic pentameter

BLAZON – a male lover describing the parts of his beloved

CADENCE – the rise of fall of sounds in a line of poetry

CAESURA – a distinct break in a poetic line, usually marked by punctuation

COMPLAINT – a type of love poem concerned with loss and mourning

CONCEIT – an extended metaphor

CONSONANCE – rhyme based on consonants only, e.g. book and back

COUPLET – a two line stanza, conventionally rhyming

DACTYL – the reverse pattern to the anapaest; stress, unstress, unstress. E.g. 'Strong as a'

DRAMATIC MONOLOGUE – a poem written in the voice of a distinct character

ELEGY – a poem in mourning for someone dead

END-RHYME – rhyming words at the end of a line

END-STOPPED – the opposite of enjambment; i.e. when the sentence and the poetic line stop at the same point

ENJAMBMENT – where sentences run over the end of lines and stanzas

FIGURATIVE LANGUAGE – language that is not literal, but employs figures of speech, such as metaphor, simile and personification

FEMININE RHYME – a rhyme that ends with an unstressed syllable or unstressed syllables.

FREE VERSE – poetry without metre or a regular, set form

GOTHIC – a style of literature characterised by psychological horror, dark deeds and uncanny events

HEROIC COUPLETS – pairs of rhymed lines in iambic pentameter

HYPERBOLE – extreme exaggeration

IAMBIC – a metrical pattern of a weak followed by a strong stress, ti-TUM, like a heart beat

IMAGERY – the umbrella term for description in poetry. Sensory imagery refers to descriptions that appeal to sight, sound and so forth; figurative imagery refers to the use of devices such as metaphor, simile and personification

JUXTAPOSITION – two things placed together to create a strong contrast

LYRIC – an emotional, personal poem usually with a first person speaker

MASCULINE RHYME – an end rhyme on a strong syllable

METAPHOR – an implicit comparison in which one thing is said to be another

METAPHYSICAL – a type of poetry characterised by wit and extended metaphors

METRE – the regular pattern organising sound and rhythm in a poem

MOTIF – a repeated image or pattern of language, often carrying thematic significance

OCTET OR OCTAVE – the opening eight lines of a sonnet

ONOMATOPOEIA – bang, crash, wallop

PENTAMETER – a poetic line consisting of five beats

PERSONIFICATION – giving human characteristics to inanimate things

PLOSIVE – a type of alliteration using 'p' and 'b' sounds

QUATRAIN – a four-line stanza

REFRAIN – a line or lines repeated like a chorus

ROMANTIC – A type of poetry characterised by a love of nature, by strong emotion and heightened tone

SESTET – the last six lines in a sonnet

SIMILE – an explicit comparison of two different things

SONNET – a form of poetry with fourteen lines and a variety of possible set rhyme patterns

SPONDEE – two strong stresses together in a line of poetry

STANZA – the technical name for a verse

SYMBOL – something that stands in for something else. Often a concrete representation of an idea.

SYNTAX – the word order in a sentence. doesn't Without sense English syntax make. Syntax is crucial to sense: For example, though it uses all the same words, 'the man eats the fish' is not the same as 'the fish eats the man'

TERCET – a three-line stanza

TETRAMETER – a line of poetry consisting of four beats

TROCHEE – the opposite of an iamb; stress, unstress, strong, weak.

VILLANELLE – a complex interlocking verse form in which lines are recycled

VOLTA – the 'turn' in a sonnet from the octave to the sestet

# Recommended reading

For the committed reader there's a brilliant overview of developments in English poetry in Part 2 of *The Oxford English Literary History, volume 12,* by Randall Stevenson.

More general books on writing, reading & analysing poetry:

Atherton, C. & Green, A. *Teaching English Literature 16-19.* NATE, 2013

Bowen et al. *The Art of Poetry, vol.1.* Peripeteia Press, 2015

Brinton, I. *Contemporary Poetry.* CUP, 2009

Eagleton, T. *How to Read a Poem.* Wiley & Sons, 2006

Fry, S. *The Ode Less Travelled.* Arrow, 2007

Heaney, S. *The Government of the Tongue.* Farrar, Straus & Giroux, 1976

Herbert, W. & Hollis, M. *Strong Words.* Bloodaxe, 2000

Meally, M. & Bowen, N. *The Art of Writing English Literature Essays,* Peripeteia Press, 2014

Maxwell, G. *On Poetry.* Oberon Masters, 2012

Padel, R. *52 Ways of Looking at a Poem.* Vintage, 2004

Padel, R. *The Poem and the Journey.* Vintage, 2008

Paulin, T. *The Secret Life of Poems.* Faber & Faber, 2011

Wolosky, S. *The Art of Poetry: How to Read a Poem.* OUP, 2008.

## Select bibliography

Bate, J. *Ted Hughes, The Unauthorised Life.* William Collins, 2016

Howarth, P. *The Cambridge Introduction to Modernist Poetry.* CUP, 2012

Hurley, M. & O'Neill, M. Poetic Form, *An Introduction.* CUP, 2012

Quinn, J. *The Cambridge Introduction to Modern Irish Poetry.* CUP, 2008.

# About the authors

An experienced Head of English and freelance writer, **Neil Bowen** is the author of many articles and resources for a range of publishers. Neil has a Masters Degree in Literature & Education from Cambridge University and he is a member of Ofqual's experts panel for English. He is the author of *The Art of Writing English Essays for GCSE* and co-author of *The Art of Writing English Essays for A-level and Beyond* and *The Art of Poetry, volume 1*. Neil also runs the peripeteia project bridging the gap between A-level and degree level English courses: www.peripeteia.webs.com

Head of A-level English, **Michael Meally**, holds an MA in American Literature as well as degrees in English Literature and Engineering. Michael's literary interests include detective/crime fiction, postcolonial literature and Greek tragedy. He is the co-author of *The Art of Writing English Literature Essays for A-level and Beyond* and *The Art of Poetry, volume 1*. Michael writes regularly for the English & Media Centre magazine.

Having studied English Language & Literature at Oxford University, where she wrote her dissertation on the opera libretti used by Benjamin Britten after the Second World War, **Johanna Harrison** will shortly begin an MA at King's College London in Nineteenth-Century Studies focusing on the intersections between European theology, literature and music. Johanna's literary interests lie particularly with the Romantic poets and late Gothicism, as well as in fin-de-siècle American literature.

**The Art of Marking -** a villanelle for English teachers

The art of marking's pretty hard to master
knowing just what and what not to write,
like writing poetry. Only somewhat harder.

Gather all the enthusiasm you can muster,
clear your mind, concentrate your might,
for the art of marking's pretty hard to master.

Sharpen those pencils, straighten the page, and after
adjust the chair, change the angle of the light.
(It's like writing poetry, only somewhat harder).

Avoid a backlog building up, you'll only feel aghaster -
piles of books toppling through dreams at night -
that part of marking's pretty hard to master.

Top tip: Better not mark books when plastered,
Those witty comments? Best keep them out of sight,
like writing poetry. It's somewhat harder

to concentrate, while swinging from the rafters,
so, settle down, quietly, your mind to the task apply.
The art of marking's pretty hard to master
Like writing poetry. Only somewhat harder.

## Answers to critical soundbites:

1. Heaney
2. Padel
3. Minhinnick
4. Turnbull (about his own poetry)
5. Thorpe
6. Flynn
7. O'Driscoll
8. Nagra
9. Ford
10. O'Brien
11. Motion
12. Szirtes (from one of his own poems)
13. Jenkins (quoting Virginia Woolf's father)
14. Morrissey

A final revision task: Students create their own anonymised critical sound bites. The class have to match the sound bite to the poet/ poem.

Critical sound bites adapted from:
https://literature.britishcouncil.org
http://www.toppingbooks.co.uk
http://www.poetryfoundation.org
http://www.forwardartsfoundation.org
http://www.theguardian.com